Jehovah's Blessing

What It Really Means
to be Blessed of God

Garry Bryant

PRESS

Table of Contents

Preface

The subject of blessing in Scripture and its present day reality is worthy of our consideration.

To be blessed, to bless, to receive a blessing; what familiar yet intriguing Biblical subjects.

They have a variety of implications and applications:

Bless the Lord;

The Lord bless you;

Be blessed;

I bless you;

In studying these words you will find a diversity of definitions and interpretations.

Bless – To receive spiritually or temporally; to be thankful; to rejoice in God's goodness; to express good or to pray over another; divine inspiration; to give honor to; granting happiness, health or prosperity; to endow with a talent or some provision; an exclamation of well-wishing; to extol or glorify.

It is obvious that this subject can have extensive implications in our lives and relationships.

Gaining a proper understanding of this whole matter can and will have tremendous positive effects upon our knowledge of and relationship with God and others.

Our purpose in this text is to investigate, define and clarify this subject using the Bible as our primary source of information.

The determined goal is to provide for you a greater perspective and understanding of God's heart and intent toward His own.

If we can capture a clearer picture of who He is, what He does and why He does it, then the time that we spend together on the journey into this subject will certainly be time well spent.

Please be informed that there is an extensive amount of Biblical passages included in this writing. This is very important and very intentional. Let us allow His Word to interpret and determine what He means when He says. . ."This is how I want to bless my people."

May the Word of God and additional text be a source of encouragement and increased revelation as to how much our great God loves you and desires to take care of you!

Enjoy!

Chapter 1

Introducing Numbers 6:22-27

The Biblical passage found in **Numbers 6:22-27** is one of the most popular and widely used of all scripture. It is commonly defined as the Priestly Blessing or the Aaronic Blessing. It is used in religious and church settings all around the world and on a regular basis.

> *The Lord said to Moses, "Tell Aaron and his sons, 'This is how you are to bless the Israelites. Say to them: ""The Lord bless you and keep you; the Lord make his face shine on you and be gracious to you; the Lord turn his face toward you and give you peace. "' "So they will put my name on the Israelites, and I will bless them."*

Many weekly church services involving a wide variety of faith expressions engage this scripture. From liturgical gatherings to charismatic worship environments, they will at some time during their public worship experience, quote, recite, declare, or pronounce this blessing. It is often used as a benediction, declaring this blessing and its provision over the people.

Too often this powerful passage of scripture has been forced into the confines of just a religious exercise or an expected part of our Church meetings.

The primary purpose of this text is to bring to a greater light the tremendous truths that are contained in this scripture and to discover in a greater way the character, desire and heart of God toward His people. To answer the question, "What does it really mean to be blessed of God?"

Many times we miss or fall short of the full content and intent of Biblical truth due to familiarity or a lack of understanding, investigation and revelation.

The Priestly Blessing is like a gold mine of truth. My goal is to help you discover the value and riches that are contained in its message and to uncover its God intended application to our lives. Golden nuggets lie in its possession; eternal truths and fresh revelation are to be found. Let's pursue and mine the wealth of truth that is contained in this powerful portion of Scripture.

It is important that in the beginning we establish the context and timing of when these words were spoken. You know the story. The children of Israel have been delivered from the bondage of Egypt and are on their way to the Promised Land. Unfortunately, this relatively short trip would take 40 years and claim the lives of the first generation of those delivered, with the exception of Joshua and Caleb.

God gives the children of Israel specific instructions and guidelines for their lifestyle and relationship with Him as His chosen people. The law was given and The Ten Commandments were delivered to Moses. It was an incredible time in their lives and history. The challenges of their journey are intriguing. Their rebellion and disobedience, which prolonged their extended stay in the wilderness, can easily remind us of our own faith journey.

The one consistent reality in that season was the ever-present mercy and love of God: He always responded with His care and provision.

So we set the scene and we see the throng of people now venturing across the desert and God has a special message for them.

Numbers 6:22-24

The Lord said to Moses, "Tell Aaron and his sons, 'This is how you are to bless the Israelites. Say to them: ""The Lord bless you and keep you;

It's extremely important that we recognize up-front that this whole blessing idea came from God. It was the <u>LORD</u> who spoke to Moses what He wanted to share with the people.

The name <u>Lord</u> identifies God as Jehovah, or in the Hebrew, Yahweh. It is very significant in the study of the Bible to discover and identify the various names of God. It is through His names that we come to a clearer understanding of the attributes and character of God. Knowing His names is one of the greatest ways to learn about Him and to know Him. It is through the names of God that He most effectively reveals

Himself to us and the relationship He wants to have with us.

The name Jehovah is one of the most prominent of His names in the Bible. It is used approximately 7,000 times in the Old Testament and referenced a number of times in the New Testament. The majority of Bible translations, or versions, do not use the word Jehovah nor Yahweh. So this name is translated and spelled LORD or GOD with all capital letters.

Before we dig into this rich vein of gold, the name Jehovah, let's for interest and benefit survey some of the other names of God we discover in the Old Testament.

ELOHIM

Strong one. It is used of God's sovereignty, creative work. It defines God as Creator, Preserver, Mighty and Strong.

Genesis 1:1

*In the beginning **God / Elohim** created the heavens and the earth.*

Genesis 1:26

*Then **God / Elohim** said, "Let us make mankind in our image, in our likeness, so that they may rule over the fish in the sea and the birds in the sky, over the livestock and all the wild animals, and over all the creatures that move along the ground."*

I Chronicles 29:10

*David praised the LORD in the presence of the whole assembly, saying, "Praise be to you, LORD, the **God / Elohim** of our father Israel, from everlasting to everlasting.*

Isaiah 45:18

*For this is what the LORD says—he who created the heavens, he is **God / Elohim**; he who fashioned and made the earth, he founded it; he did not create it to be empty, but formed it to be inhabited—he says: "I am the LORD, and there is no other.*

Jeremiah 31:33

*"This is the covenant I will make with the people of Israel after that time," declares the LORD. "I will put my law in their minds and write it on their hearts. I will be their **God / Elohim**, and they will be my people.*

EL-SHADDAI

God Almighty, the Lord God, the Almighty God, Omnipotent One, all Sufficient One, all Bountiful One. The Almighty God who can carry out His purpose and plans to their fullest completion.

Genesis 17:1-2

*When Abram was ninety-nine years old, the L*ORD *appeared to him and said, "I am **God Almighty / El-Shaddai**; walk before me faithfully and be blameless. Then I will make my covenant between me and you and will greatly increase your numbers."*

Genesis 28:3

*May **God Almighty / El-Shaddai** bless you and make you fruitful and increase your numbers until you become a community of peoples.*

Psalm 91:1

*Whoever dwells in the shelter of the Most High will rest in the shadow of the **Almighty/El-Shaddai**.*

Isaiah 60:16

*Then you will know that I, the L*ORD*, am your Savior, your Redeemer, the **Mighty One / El-Shaddai** of Jacob.*

EL-ELYON

The Most Holy God. God of strength and supremacy. The God who has no equal. The highly-exalted, sovereign God.

Genesis 14:18-20 and 22

Then Melchizedek king of Salem brought out bread and wine. He was priest of **God Most High / El-Elyon***, and he blessed Abram, saying, "Blessed be Abram by* **God Most High / El-Elyon***, Creator of heaven and earth. And praise be to* **God Most High / El-Elyon***, who delivered your enemies into your hand."*

But Abram said to the king of Sodom, "With raised hand I have sworn an oath to the Lord*,* **God Most High / El-Elyon***, Creator of heaven and earth*

Psalm 9:2

I will be glad and rejoice in you; I will sing the praises of your name, **O Most High / El Elyon***.*

Psalm 78:35

They remembered that **God / El-Elyon** *was their Rock, that God Most High was their Redeemer.*

Daniel 3:26

Nebuchadnezzar then approached the opening of the blazing furnace and shouted, "Shadrach, Meshach and Abednego, servants of the **Most High God / El-Elyon***, come out! Come here!"*

So Shadrach, Meshach and Abednego came out of the fire

Daniel 4:2-3

*It is my pleasure to tell you about the miraculous signs and wonders that the **Most High God / El-Elyon** has performed for me. How great are his signs, how mighty his wonders! His kingdom is an eternal kingdom; his dominion endures from generation to generation.*

EL-OLAM

The Everlasting God. The God of Ages. The eternal, unchanging One.

Psalm 90:2

*Before the mountains were born or you brought forth the whole world, from everlasting to everlasting you are **God / El-Olam**.*

Isaiah 40:28

*Do you not know? Have you not heard? The L*ORD *is the everlasting **God / El-Olam**, the Creator of the ends of the earth. He will not grow tired or weary, and his understanding no one can fathom.*

Isaiah 63:16

But you are our Father, though Abraham does not know us or Israel acknowledge us; you, Lord / El-Olam, are our Father, our Redeemer from of old is your name.

Jeremiah 10:10

*But the Lord is the true **God / El-Olam**; he is the living God, the eternal King. When he is angry, the earth trembles; the nations cannot endure his wrath.*

Romans 16:25-26

*Now to him who is able to establish you in accordance with my gospel, the message I proclaim about Jesus Christ, in keeping with the revelation of the mystery hidden for long ages past, but now revealed and made known through the prophetic writings by the command of the eternal **God / El-Olam**, so that all the Gentiles might come to the obedience that comes from faith*

I Timothy 1:17

*Now to the King eternal, immortal, invisible, the only **God / El-Olam**, be honor and glory for ever and ever. Amen.*

ADONAI

God is Lord, Ruler, Sovereign. This name emphasizes the Lordship of God.

Genesis 15:2

But Abram said, "Sovereign **LORD /** **Adonai**, *what can you give me since I remain childless and the one who will inherit my estate is Eliezer of Damascus?"*

Exodus 20:7

You shall not misuse the name of the Lord your **God / Adonai**, *for the Lord will not hold anyone guiltless who misuses his name.*

Judges 3:8

The anger of the **Lord / Adonai** *burned against Israel so that he sold them into the hands of Cushan-Rishathaim King of Aram Naharaim, to whom the Israelites were subject for eight years.*

Nehemiah 1:11

Lord / Adonai, *let your ear be attentive to the prayer of this your servant and to the prayer of your servants who delight in revering your name. Give your servant success today by granting him favor in the presence of this man.*

El-Roi

The God who continually sees.

Genesis 16:13

*She gave this name to the LORD who spoke to her: "You are the **God / El-Roi** who sees me," for she said, "I have now seen the **One / El-Roi** who sees me."*

2 Chronicles 16:9

*For the eyes of the **LORD / El-Roi** range throughout the earth to strengthen those whose hearts are fully committed to him. You have done a foolish thing, and from now on you will be at war. "*

Psalm 33:18-19

*But the eyes of the **LORD / El-Roi** are on those who fear him, on those whose hope is in his unfailing love, [to] deliver them from death and keep them alive in famine.*

Psalm 34:15

*The eyes of the **LORD / El-Roi** are on the righteous, and his ears are attentive to their cry.*

Now let's return to the name Jehovah. . .

Jehovah

The self-existent One who is personal and relational.

Exodus 4:5

*"This," said the **Lord / Jehovah**, "is so that they may believe that the **Lord / Jehovah**, the God of their fathers – the God of Abraham, the God of Isaac and the God of Jacob – has appeared to you."*

Nehemiah 9:3

*They stood where they were and read from the Book of the Law of the **Lord their God / Jehovah** for a quarter of the day, and spent another quarter in confession and in worshiping the **Lord their God / Jehovah**.*

Psalm 30:12

*That my heart may sing your praises and not be silent. **Lord my God / Jehovah**, I will praise you forever.*

Isaiah 14:24

*The **Lord Almighty / Jehovah** has sworn, "Surely, as I have planned, so it will be, and as I have purposed, so it will happen."*

As you can imagine, this is not an exhaustive list nor is it an extensive explanation of the Old Testament names of God. It is but limited evidence of the purpose, along with the significance of how God revealed Himself through His name. The various names of God are like viewing the brilliance and uniqueness of a multi-faceted diamond. Each angle has its own beauty as well as its own distinction, but all the same gemstone. This certainly encourages us to Bless His Holy Name!

Let us maintain our focus on the name Jehovah. There are many variations of this name with many definitions. They all derive from the basis of the eternal existence of God and that He is the one who brings all things into existence. The self-existent God of revelation, relationship and redemption.

One of the more popular references to this name is found in Exodus 3; the experience of Moses at the burning bush. What an intriguing setting, which included a most interesting conversation taking place between God and the soon to be deliverer, Moses.

Exodus 3:1-15

Now Moses was tending the flock of Jethro his father-in-law, the priest of Midian, and he led the flock to the far side of the wilderness and came to Horeb, the mountain of God. There the angel of the LORD appeared to him in flames of fire from within a bush. Moses saw that though the bush was on fire it did not burn up. So Moses thought, "I will go over and see this strange sight—why the bush does not burn up."

*When the **LORD / JEHOVAH** saw that he had gone over to look, God called to him from within the bush, "Moses! Moses!"*

And Moses said, "Here I am."

"Do not come any closer," God said. "Take off your sandals, for the place where you are standing is holy ground." Then he said, "I am the God of your father, the God of Abraham, the God of Isaac and the God of Jacob." At this, Moses hid his face, because he was afraid to look at God.

*The **LORD / JEHOVAH** said, "I have indeed seen the misery of my people in Egypt. I have heard them crying out because of their slave drivers, and I am concerned about their suffering. So I have come down to rescue them from the hand of the Egyptians and to bring them up out of that land into a good and spacious land, a land flowing with milk and honey—the home of the Canaanites, Hittites, Amorites, Perizzites, Hivites and Jebusites. And now the cry of the Israelites has reached me, and I have seen the way the Egyptians are oppressing them. So now, go. I am sending you to Pharaoh to bring my people the Israelites out of Egypt."*

But Moses said to God, "Who am I that I should go to Pharaoh and bring the Israelites out of Egypt?"

And God said, "I will be with you. And this will be the sign to you that it is I who have sent you: When you have brought the people out of Egypt, you will worship God on this mountain. "

Moses said to God, "Suppose I go to the Israelites and say to them, 'The God of your fathers has sent me to you,' and they ask me, 'What is his name?' Then what shall I tell them?"

God said to Moses, "I AM WHO I AM. This is what you are to say to the Israelites: 'I AM has sent me to you.'"

*God also said to Moses, "Say to the Israelites, '**The LORD / JEHOVAH**, the God of your fathers—the God of Abraham, the God of Isaac and the God of Jacob— has sent me to you.' "This is my name forever, <u>the name you shall call me from generation to generation.</u>*

It is very important during our visit with this passage that we discern the heart and characteristics of God. He is revealing Himself and defining Himself as Jehovah. We can see His mercy, compassion and His attentiveness to the peoples cry, suffering and bondage. The God who responds to His people, who is faithful to His promises and who goes with and helps those He sends.

In verse 13, Moses requests greater validation and identification. He is asking God for His name. God, in verse 14, provides the answer which is the most familiar part of this whole passage. "I AM WHO I AM – the I AM has sent you." This is the most consistent definition of the name Jehovah. "I AM WHO I AM" or "I AM THAT I AM", the "I AM".

Exodus 3:15

> *God also said to Moses, "Say to the Israelites, 'The LORD / JEHOVAH, the God of your fathers—the God of Abraham, the God of Isaac and the God of Jacob—has sent me to you.' "This is my name forever, the name you shall call me from generation to generation."*

He is the all-sufficient one, self-existent one. He is constant, unchanging, faithful, sure and true. He is Jehovah! Giving full evidence that He is concerned for His people and committed to their redemption.

There is another important scriptural passage to consider when pursuing the identity and characteristics of God as Jehovah. The account is found in Exodus chapters 33 and 34. In verse eighteen of chapter 33, Moses asked to see the glory of God. In verse nineteen, the LORD responds by saying, "*I will cause all my goodness to pass in front of you and I will proclaim my name, the LORD in your presence.*

I will have mercy on whom I will have mercy, and I will have compassion on whom I will have compassion." In **Exodus 34:5-8**, we see this prayer and promise fulfilled.

> *Then the **LORD** / **JEHOVAH** came down in the cloud and stood there with him and proclaimed his name, the **LORD** / **JEHOVAH**. And he passed in front of Moses, proclaiming, "The LORD / JEHOVAH, the **LORD** / **JEHOVAH**, the compassionate and gracious God, slow to anger, abounding in love and faithfulness, maintaining love to thousands, and forgiving wickedness, rebellion and sin. Yet he does not leave the guilty unpunished; he punishes the children and their children for the sin of the parents to the third and fourth generation." Moses bowed to the ground at once and worshiped.*

Here Jehovah reveals Himself as compassionate, gracious, slow to anger, loving, faithful, forgiving, full of righteousness and justice. WOW! What a powerful revelation of Who He is and what tremendous insight to His attributes, actions and characteristics.

It is my observation in studying and searching out this particular name of God, that it could be adequately defined as the Old Testament redemptive name of God and reveals Him as a relational God. Not just a God of great power, not just a creative God, not just a God of supremacy and strength, not just a God who has no equal, not just a God who is eternal and self-sufficient, but a God who has intentionally and consistently revealed Himself as He who wants to love, forgive, redeem and who wants to be in relationship with His creation. This is more clearly understood by considering the compound names of Jehovah that we discover throughout the Old Testament.

Jehovah Jireh – The LORD will provide **Genesis 22:14**

Jehovah Nissi – The LORD is my banner **Exodus 17:15**

Jehovah Shalom – The LORD is my peace **Judges 6:24**

Jehovah Sabbaoth – The LORD of Hosts **I Samuel 1:3**

Jehovah M'Kaddesh – The LORD, your sanctifier **Exodus 31:13**

Jehovah Rohi – The LORD my shepherd **Psalm 23:1**

Jehovah Tsidkenu – The LORD our righteousness **Jeremiah 23:6**

Jehovah Shammah – The LORD is there **Exodus 48:35**

Jehovah Raphe – The LORD who heals **Exodus 15:22-26**

Each of these names give distinct and additional validation as to how God wants us to understand His heart, character and available provision. God wants to be involved in our lives. He wants to provide for us, heal us, protect us, impart His character in us, and be with us. Jehovah God wants to be our shepherd, as well as our peace: He has promised us the victory. Amazing!

Psalm 103 is a wonderful description of Jehovah!

> *Praise the **LORD / JEVOVAH**, my soul; all my inmost being, praise his holy name. Praise the **LORD / JEHOVAH**, my soul, and forget not all his benefits—who <u>forgives</u> all your sins and <u>heals</u> all your diseases, who <u>redeems</u> your life from the pit and <u>crowns</u> you with <u>love</u> and <u>compassion</u>, who <u>satisfies</u> your desires with good things so that your youth is renewed like the eagle's. The **LORD / JEHOVAH** works <u>righteousness</u> and <u>justice</u> for all the oppressed. He made known his ways to Moses, his deeds to the people of Israel: The **LORD / JEHOVAH** is <u>compassionate</u> and <u>gracious</u>, <u>slow to anger</u>, <u>abounding in love</u>. He will not always accuse, nor will he harbor his anger forever; he does not treat us as our sins deserve or repay us according to our iniquities. For as high as the heavens are above the earth, <u>so great is his love</u> for those who fear him; as far as the east is from the west, so far has he removed our transgressions from us. As*

*a father has <u>compassion</u> on his children,
so the **Lord / Jehovah** has <u>compassion</u> on
those who fear him; for he knows how
we are formed, he remembers that we
are dust. The life of mortals is like grass,
they flourish like a flower of the field;
the wind blows over it and it is gone,
and its place remembers it no more. But
from everlasting to everlasting the **Lord's
/ JEHOVAH's** <u>love</u> is with those who
fear him, and his <u>righteousness</u> with
their children's children—with those who
keep his covenant and remember to obey
his precepts. The **Lord / Jehovah** has
established his throne in heaven, and his
kingdom rules over all. Praise the **Lord /
Jehovah**, you his angels, you mighty ones
who do his bidding, who obey his word.
Praise the **Lord / Jehovah**, all his heavenly
hosts, you his servants who do his will.
Praise the **Lord / Jehovah**, all his works
everywhere in his dominion. Praise the
Lord / Jehovah, my soul.*

What a powerful declaration and revelation of Jehovah. The God who redeems and
who desires to be in relationship with you!
Hallelujah!

Now let us look back to the passage in
Numbers 6. The LORD said to Moses. . . We
can more effectively and accurately understand
the continuation of this text now that we have a
clear understanding of the one who is initiating
and declaring this blessing.

The Lord communicates to His primary leader, Moses. He instructs him to inform Aaron and his sons of their responsibility to impart this blessing to the people of Israel. This instruction is very important to Jehovah's overall intent and purpose. This was not just a religious exercise or heavenly verbiage. It was to be a revelation of His heart toward His people and to serve as a source of Divine intent and impartation.

Chapter 2

The Lord Bless You?

Numbers 6:23

"Tell Aaron and his sons, 'This is how you are to bless the Israelites. . .

J ehovah is providing specific instructions as to how He wants this spiritual responsibility and heavenly provision carried out. He is very intentional in regards to the blessing He desired to be released and imparted over the Israelites. As is obvious, God has a particular plan relative to this blessing.

Psalm 67:1-2

May God be gracious to us and bless us and make his face shine on us—so that your ways may be known on earth, your salvation among all nations.

The whole concept of blessing is a very familiar yet unique Biblical subject. There is much said about blessing but unfortunately a limited understanding. You cannot separate the blessings of God from the purpose of God, as this verse from Psalm 67 clearly states.

The Psalmist said in his prayer, *"Be gracious to us and bless us. Make Your face shine upon us."* Why? There is a reason. Not for my selfish absorption, not just for my personal gain. But the primary reason that is connected to the blessings of God is that His ways may be known on the earth declaring His salvation among all nations.

When we acknowledge the blessings of God upon our lives, we must come under the immediate responsibility that in those blessings is the duty and privilege of using the blessings of God as an instrument of carrying out His purpose in the earth; which is making His salvation known.

As Christians, we are consistently blessing others in our conversations. To say "The LORD bless you" is a regular part of our way of speaking. We use that phrase in a variety of ways and it brings with it a very pleasing sense of God's involvement and a level of care from the individual who is speaking. We say "The LORD bless you" in greeting friends, strangers, fellow believers, and almost everyone. It is used to open conversations along with closing them. We use this phrase as a source of encouragement, a means of prayer and in a variety of ways in a variety of settings. It is a very common, appropriate and acceptable part of our Christian communication.

Another familiar use of the term "bless" or "blessed" is just as interesting. Many times when a believer is asked "How are you doing", the reply will be "I am blessed of the Lord", or simply, "I am blessed". This again is a common practice and an indication of one's faith and understanding of God's involvement in their lives.

We often hear phrases such as:

> I am blessed and highly favored
> I am too blessed to be distressed
> I am blessed above the rest
> I am blessed by the best

These ring with recognition of God's provision.

The question that I want to raise, and the question that will provide the primary basis for this writing is: <u>What does it really mean to be blessed of the Lord?</u> What is one really saying when the statement made is: "I am blessed"? What is being said when one declares "The Lord bless you"?

I have found it extremely intriguing when these questions are raised among Christians. My discovery has been that most have never given it much consideration, certainly very little investigation. What is the real truth of these very familiar words and Christian terminology? The responses to these kinds of questions are about as distinct as the individuals answering.

Typically, the understanding or definition revolves around that which is tangible. I am blessed because I have a good job or a positive income. I am blessed because I have a good retirement or some level of positive finances. I am blessed because I have a good family, great spouse and respectable children. I am blessed because I have a house, car, food and clothes. I am blessed because I live in America or some other favorable part of the world. I am blessed because I am healthy, or do not have any particular physical problem. I am blessed because. . .(you can complete the sentence).

This has become the primary and popular way to explain the blessing of God.

It proves to be very challenging when you consider this subject from a Biblical perspective to connect the true meaning of the blessing of God with those things that are only tangible, natural and physical.

As we progress in this subject, we will discover that they can play a role in God's blessing, however they cannot be the total definition or the true evidence of what the Bible truly means when Jehovah says, "This is how I want to bless my people."

Let's look at the flip-side of this popular and preferred explanation of God's blessing, or what it means to be blessed.

If the blessing of God is evidenced and proven by things, possessions, or the abundance of physical provision, what does that say about those who do not have the same testimony? What about the faith-filled, God-fearing believers that have less than? Are they not blessed by God or not as blessed as those who have more?

Oh, I realize that this goes against the grain of much contemporary preachings, teachings and religious practices. I am very aware that this refutes the ideas and philosophy that the favor and blessing of God is proven primarily by my possessions and the level of high-living and economic success I can obtain.

Without question this will generate opposition from the "bless me" club and those who have chosen to make faith and favor a deceptive way to heap upon themselves the very things of which Jesus warned us.

How can the blessing of God be degraded to things when Jesus informed us that life does not consist of the abundance of things? How can the blessing of God be required to mean primarily financial prosperity when it is Jesus who warns us that wealth makes it very difficult to get to heaven? This is clearly communicated in Jesus' encounter with the rich young man in **Matthew 19:16-24.**

> *Just then a man came up to Jesus and asked, "Teacher, what good thing must I do to get eternal life?" "Why do you ask me about what is good?" Jesus replied. "There is only One who is good. If you want to enter life, keep the commandments." "Which ones?" he inquired. Jesus replied, "'You shall not murder, you shall not commit adultery, you shall not steal, you shall not give false testimony, honor your father and mother and 'love your neighbor as yourself.'" "All these I have kept," the young man said. "What do I still lack?" Jesus answered, "If you want to be perfect, go, sell your possessions and give to the poor, and you will have treasure in heaven. Then come, follow me." When the young man heard this, he*

*went away sad, because he had great
wealth. <u>Then Jesus said to his disciples,
"Truly I tell you, it is hard for someone
who is rich to enter the kingdom of
heaven. Again I tell you, it is easier for a
camel to go through the eye of a needle
than for someone who is rich to enter the
kingdom of God."</u>*

Let's un-package this some more and make
the necessary effort to simplify and clarify what
it does and does not mean to be blessed of God.

Can the blessing of God mean what we have
allowed it to become? An essential aspect of
proper Biblical interpretation is that truth is
universal. Truth must be allowed and required
to apply to all people: every race, creed, color,
tongue, nation and people group. If it is truth
in one place then it is truth everywhere; every
continent and in every country, and for all
people. Truth is the same. Truth does not
change based on culture, location, economic
status or any other distinguishing feature
of mankind.

Truth is truth! This is a fundamental aspect
of determining proper Biblical understanding
and application.

I am afraid that the Westernized, America-
nized, popularized definition of the blessing of
God is warped and it improperly interprets the
heart of God and intent of Scripture.

If the prosperous, the more successful, the
well-to-do are the more blessed, what about the
majority of the world's population that cannot
make this claim or have such a testimony?

What about the faithful men and women of God who have meager means and many who live in abstract poverty? Would we say that they are not blessed of God? What about those who worship in very limited sanctuaries or even outdoors because they cannot afford a church building? Are they not as blessed as those of us who are privileged and even spoiled by our beautiful buildings and our expensive and expansive places of worship? Could we possibly say that a wealthy individual is more blessed than the saints of God who do not have?

Obviously there is something off-center with our present day theology and application of the Blessing of God. Without question, our emphasis on tangible prosperity and our description of God's favor has polluted and diluted God's intent and purpose in how He has chosen to bless His people.

It is doing the Scripture an injustice and applying improper interpretation to defile and devalue the role of God's blessing to that which can be primarily determined by natural and physical measurements.

How does our present day application of God's blessing apply to the life of the Apostle Paul or even to Christ Himself? Would we dare say that Paul was not blessed? Yet he made the following observations of his Christian journey and ministry.

2 Corinthians 4

Therefore, since through God's mercy we have this ministry, we do not lose heart.

43

Rather, we have renounced secret and shameful ways; we do not use deception, nor do we distort the word of God. On the contrary, by setting forth the truth plainly we commend ourselves to everyone's conscience in the sight of God. And even if our gospel is veiled, it is veiled to those who are perishing. The god of this age has blinded the minds of unbelievers, so that they cannot see the light of the gospel that displays the glory of Christ, who is the image of God. For what we preach is not ourselves, but Jesus Christ as Lord, and ourselves as your servants for Jesus' sake. For God, who said, "Let light shine out of darkness," made his light shine in our hearts to give us the light of the knowledge of God's glory displayed in the face of Christ. But we have this treasure in jars of clay to show that this all-surpassing power is from God and not from us. We are hard pressed on every side, but not crushed; perplexed, but not in despair; persecuted, but not abandoned; struck down, but not destroyed. We always carry around in our body the death of Jesus, so that the life of Jesus may also be revealed in our body. For we who are alive are always being given over to death for Jesus' sake, so that his life may also be revealed in our mortal body. So then, death is at work in us, but life is at work in you. It is written: "I believed; therefore I have spoken." Since we have that same spirit of faith, we also believe and therefore speak, because we know that the one who raised the Lord Jesus from the dead will also raise us with Jesus and present us with you to himself. All this is for your benefit, so that the grace that is reaching more and more people may cause thanksgiving to overflow to the glory of God. Therefore we do not lose heart. Though outwardly we are wasting away, yet inwardly we are being renewed day by day. For our light and momentary troubles are achieving for us an eternal glory that far outweighs them all. So we fix our eyes not on what is seen, but on what is unseen, since what is seen is temporary, but what is unseen is eternal.

2 Corinthians 6:1-10

As God's co-workers we urge you not to receive God's grace in vain. For he says, "In the time of my favor I heard you, and in the day of salvation I helped you." I tell you, now is the time of God's favor, now is the day of salvation. We put no stumbling block in anyone's path, so that our ministry will not be discredited. Rather, as servants of God we commend ourselves in every way: in great endurance; in troubles, hardships and distresses; in beatings, imprisonments and riots; in hard work, sleepless nights and hunger; in purity, understanding, patience and kindness; in the Holy Spirit and in sincere love; in truthful speech and in the power of God; with weapons of righteousness in the right hand and in the left; through glory and dishonor, bad report and good report; genuine, yet regarded as impostors; known, yet regarded as unknown; dying, and yet we live on; beaten, and yet not killed; sorrowful, yet always rejoicing; poor, yet making many rich; having nothing, and yet possessing everything.

2 Corinthians 11:22-27

Are they Hebrews? So am I. Are they Israelites? So am I. Are they Abraham's descendants? So am I. Are they servants of Christ? (I am out of my mind to talk like this.) I am more. I have worked much harder, been in prison more frequently, been flogged more severely, and been exposed to death again and again. Five times I received from the Jews the forty lashes minus one. Three times I was beaten with rods, once I was pelted with stones, three times I was shipwrecked, I spent a night and a day in the open sea, I have been constantly on the move. I have been in danger from rivers, in danger from bandits, in danger from my fellow Jews, in danger from Gentiles; in danger in the city, in danger in the country, in danger at sea; and in danger from false believers. I have labored and toiled and have often gone without sleep; I have known hunger and thirst and have often gone without food; I have been cold and naked.

Amazing, isn't it? Certainly the great New Testament leader and author, the Apostle to the Gentiles, would declare that he was blessed of God. He did so many times and in a variety of ways throughout his anointed writings. But how he defined "blessing" would not fit into the present day interpretation and application.

Was it not Christ who made the claim that He did not even have a place to lay His head?

Matthew 8:20

Jesus replied, "Foxes have dens and birds have nests, but the Son of Man has no place to lay his head."

Let's remind ourselves of Christ's teaching in the Sermon on the Mount.

Matthew 6:25-34

"Therefore I tell you, do not worry about your life, what you will eat or drink; or about your body, what you will wear. Is not life more than food, and the body more than clothes? Look at the birds of the air; they do not sow or reap or store away in barns, and yet your heavenly Father feeds them. Are you not much more valuable than they? Can any one of you by worrying add a single hour to your life? "And why do you worry about

clothes? See how the flowers of the field grow. They do not labor or spin. Yet I tell you that not even Solomon in all his splendor was dressed like one of these. If that is how God clothes the grass of the field, which is here today and tomorrow is thrown into the fire, will he not much more clothe you—you of little faith? So do not worry, saying, 'What shall we eat?' or 'What shall we drink?' or 'What shall we wear?' For the pagans run after all these things, and your heavenly Father knows that you need them. But seek first his kingdom and his righteousness, and all these things will be given to you as well. Therefore do not worry about tomorrow, for tomorrow will worry about itself. Each day has enough trouble of its own.

Does this sound like the popular teachings of today in regards to the proof of the favor and blessing of God? Does Christ's instruction validate the emphasis that is being placed on the pursuit of things and the emphasis on possessions, wealth and social status?

Was it not Christ that required us to recognize the cost of being a Disciple and even the sacrifice that it demands? This whole dynamic of Christianity is seemingly lost in today's Christian philosophy and teachings.

Luke 14:25-34

Large crowds were traveling with Jesus, and turning to them he said: "If anyone comes to me and does not hate father and *mother, wife and children, brothers and* *sisters—yes, even their own life—such a* *person cannot be my disciple. And who-ever does not carry their cross and follow me cannot be my disciple. "Suppose one of you wants to build a tower. Won't you first sit down and estimate the cost to see if you have enough money to complete it? For if you lay the foundation and are not able to finish it, everyone who sees it will ridicule you, saying, 'This person began to build and wasn't able to finish.' "Or suppose a king is about to go to war against another king. Won't he first sit down and consider whether he is able with ten thousand men to oppose the one coming against him with twenty thousand? If he is not able, he will send a delegation while the other is still a long way off and will ask for terms of peace.* *In the same way, those of you who do not give up everything you have cannot be my disciples. "Salt is good, but if it loses its saltiness, how can it be made salty again?*

There must be a correction to our modern interpretation. We must believe for proper Biblical understanding. May the Holy Spirit provide for us fresh revelation in regards to the Biblical theme of God's blessing. May He lead us into all truth. . .teach us! I pray we be willing to allow God's genuine and original intent of blessing His people be discovered and received.

I, with you, joyfully declare I am blessed of God! I also want to declare the blessings of God over your life, family, home, profession, health, finances, ministry, future, etc. But what does that really mean? What is Biblically being established, asked, and released? What an amazing subject!

Let's continue surveying this whole concept.

Are you aware of what God's first action was after He created Adam and Eve? Re-visit with me the scene. We must begin at the beginning. God is in creation mode. *"And God said."* Then there was light, land, water, the sky, vegetation. WOW!

Not only did God speak, but He looked and saw that it was good. God spoke and there was the sun, moon, every living creature in the water and on the land. He saw it and again declared it was good.

Genesis 1:26-27

> *Then God said, "Let us make mankind in our image, in our likeness, so that they may rule over the fish in the sea and the birds in the sky, over the livestock and all the wild animals, and over all the creatures that move along the ground." So God created mankind in his own image, in the image of God he created them; male and female he created them.*

The creation of man: God's final creative act during six days of unbelievable yet undeniable activity. So, we have this creative genius, God, exercising His miraculous capacity, unlimited potential and supernatural creativity. Everything He spoke came into existence and in its perfected form. As already referenced, He observed, analyzed and declared it all good.

In verse 31 of Genesis one, it states that He saw all that He had made and it was very good. God's "very good" could be defined as perfect. A perfect God creating a perfect world and placing in it two perfect people. Sounds like a good situation. How can you improve on perfection?

Now let's visit **Genesis 1:27-28**.

<u>God blessed them</u> and said to them, "Be fruitful and increase in number; fill the earth and subdue it. Rule over the fish in the sea and the birds in the sky and over every living creature that moves on the ground. "

The first three words will be our emphasis. "God blessed them. . ." What? Are you kidding me? What does that mean? What could that mean? In all of this creative perfection, God blesses them. What did He do? What more could He do? How do you add to or improve on Divine Perfection?

What action did God take? What promise did He make? Was it some verbal declaration? Was it something He gave them? Was it something He physically did for them? It proves very intriguing. He blessed them! We will answer these questions a little later on.

Genesis is filled with this activity of God. The words blessed, bless, and blessing are found approximately 75 times in the first book of the Bible.

There are many familiar Biblical characters and accounts where this matter of the blessing continues to dominate the action of God, His relationship with man and the activity of Scripture.

God blessed Adam and Eve. Genesis 1:28; Genesis 5;2
God blessed Noah and his sons. Genesis 9:1
God blessed Abraham. Genesis 12:2-3; Genesis 17; Genesis 24:1; Genesis 26:24
God Blessed Sarah. Genesis 17:15-16
God blessed Ishmael. Genesis 17:20

One of the dominating aspects of the Abrahamic Covenant flows out of the promise of God to bless not only Abraham and his family, but all of those that will bless him and his seed. We see this blessing being transferred to his son, Isaac, and to the generations that followed: That all the nations of the earth would be blessed.

It is obvious from the writings of Genesis, as well as the continued emphasis of God blessing his people throughout Scripture, that this would be a consistent theme in regards to how He desires to relate to His people.

Let us look at and reference the subjects of bless, blessed, and blessing as they are discovered in the Bible

- Individuals (Gen. 32:29)
- Fruit of the Womb (Deut. 7:13)
- Crops of your land (Deut. 4:2)
- Labors (Deut. 15:10)
- In the City (Deut. 28:3)
- In the Country (Deut. 28:3)
- Harvest (Deut. 28:4)
- Livestock (Deut. 28:4)
- When you come in (Deut. 28:6)
- When you go out (Deut. 28:6)
- Work of your hands (Deut. 28:8)
- Land (Deut. 28:8)
- Household (2 Samuel 6:11)
- The Righteous (Psalm 5:12)
- Inheritance (Psalm 28:9)
- Whose transgressions are forgiven (Psalm 32:1)
- He who comes in the Name of the Lord (Psalm 118:26)
- Those who fear the Lord (Psalm 128:1)
- In battle (Psalm 144:1)
- Nations (Jeremiah 4:2)
- Those who trust in the Lord (Jeremiah 17:7)
- Poor in spirit (Matthew 5:3)
- Those who mourn (Matthew 5:4)
- The meek (Matthew 5:5)
- Those who hunger and thirst for righteousness (Matthew 5:6)
- The merciful (Matthew 5:7)
- The pure in heart (Matthew 5:8)
- Peacemakers (Matthew 5:9)
- Those who are persecuted (Matthew 5:10)
- All people (Acts 3:25)

Deuteronomy 28:1-14

*If you fully obey the L*ORD *your God and carefully follow all his commands I give you today, the L*ORD *your God will set you high above all the nations on earth. All these* <u>blessings</u> *will come on you and accompany you if you obey the L*ORD *your God: You will be* <u>blessed</u> *in the city and* <u>blessed</u> *in the country. The fruit of your womb will be* <u>blessed</u>*, and the crops of your land and the young of your live-stock—the calves of your herds and the lambs of your flocks. Your basket and your kneading trough will be* <u>blessed</u>*. You will be* <u>blessed</u> *when you come in and* <u>blessed</u> *when you go out. The L*ORD *will grant that the enemies who rise up against you will be defeated before you. They will come at you from one direction but flee from you in seven. The L*ORD *will send a* <u>blessing</u> *on your barns and on everything you put your hand to. The L*ORD *your God will* <u>bless</u> *you in the land he is giving you. The L*ORD *will establish you as his holy people, as he promised you on oath, if you keep the commands of the L*ORD *your God and walk in obedience to him. Then all the peoples on earth will see that you are called by the name of the L*ORD*, and they will fear you. The L*ORD *will grant you abundant prosperity—in the fruit of your womb, the young of your livestock and the crops of your ground— in the land he swore to your ancestors to* *give you. The LORD will open the heavens, the storehouse of his bounty, to send rain on your land in season and to <u>bless</u> all the work of your hands. You will lend to many nations but will borrow from none. The LORD will make you the head, not the tail. If you pay attention to the commands of the LORD your God that I give you this day and carefully follow them, you will always be at the top, never at the bottom. Do not turn aside from any of the commands I give you today, to the right or to the left, following other gods and serving them.*

Psalm 128

<u>Blessed</u> are all who fear the LORD, who walk in obedience to him. You will eat the fruit of your labor; <u>blessings</u> and prosperity will be yours. Your wife will be like a fruitful vine within your house; your children will be like olive shoots around your table. Yes, this will be the <u>blessing</u> for the man who fears the LORD. May the LORD <u>bless</u> you from Zion; may you see the prosperity of Jerusalem all the days of your life. May you live to see your children's children—peace be on Israel.

This activity of God wanting to bless; providing His blessing; promising to bless, is without question a very attractive aspect of His character. It is a compelling dynamic of His determined relationship with His people.

The previous Scriptures are by no means an exhaustive list, instead are but a sampling of how this subject is presented Biblically.

How amazing is God's love, care desires and promises. The reality of the blessing of God and being blessed by God encompasses our lives with such broad and diverse potential. It is obvious as you study this subject throughout the entirety of Scripture, that blessing is a direct decision and action of God and is in direct connection with our relationship and obedience to Him.

Chapter 3

What Does It Really Mean?

In order for us to move forward effectively in the understanding and explanations of our primary emphasis: Jehovah's Blessing; Numbers 6:22-27, we must consider the following very seriously. This will establish the basis of our continuation and will bring clarification to our theme.

The word "*bless*" in the Old Testament is the Hebrew word "*barak*" – which means "to kneel" – it carries the connotation of bringing a gift on bended knee. It carries the idea of being strengthened in weakness – being compensated with God's strength, an empowerment from God to be able to do what is not within our capacity or capabilities.

Numbers 6:23

"Tell Aaron and his sons, 'This is how you are to bless the Israelites. Say to them:

In aggressively pursuing the meaning and application of the Biblical subject of blessing, we must give opportunity for the entirety of Scripture to be involved. We must allow the original intent of the Biblical language to be given priority consideration. We must observe and define the subject in light of the character and heart of God.

As noted earlier in this writing, the whole idea of bless, blessed and blessing was God's. He originated this action during the days of creation and it continues to be His heart and action toward man today.

The blessing of God simply means that He comes to us as if on bended knee and presents Himself even as a servant; offering us provision and heaven's supply based on His purpose, plan and will for our lives. It is as if He comes to you, kneels before you, looks you in the eyes and asks, "What can I do for you? What do you need? How can I serve you?" This is an amazing portrait of a loving, caring, generous and providing God. Remember He presented Himself in this setting as Jehovah. He is compassionate, gracious, patient, loving, faithful, forgiving, righteous and just.

Is not the position and practice of servant-hood heaven's model for life? Did not Jesus, in fulfilling and revealing the pure heart of God in word and deed declare, "I have not come to be served, but to serve"? Did He not teach us that in order for us to be the greatest, we must be the servant of all? Does it not make Biblical sense that God's heart toward His people is to come to them on an individual basis and position Himself to serve them by providing for them, taking care of them and meeting their needs? Is not true leadership, Biblical leadership, Godly leadership taking on the posture and action of a servant? The Lord Jehovah wants to bless you! He wants to serve you! He wants to labor, provide, serve, and care for you. Amazing! There is no god like our God!

We see this whole concept presented and validated as He revealed Himself through these compound names of Jehovah. Be reminded how He presents Himself.

Jehovah Jireh – He is your Provider!
Jehovah Nissi – He is your Banner!
Jehovah Shalom – He is your Peace!
Jehovah Sabbaoth – He is to you the Lord of Hosts!
Jehovah M'Kaddesh – He is your Sanctifier!
Jehovah Rohi – He is your Shepherd!
Jehovah Tsidkenu – He is your Righteousness!
Jehovah Shammah – He is always There for you!
Jehovah Raphe – He is your Healer!

God is saying to us, "I am here on your behalf. I have what you need and anxiously desire to provide for you. I am present to serve you!"

For many, this is difficult to receive, hard to understand and unreasonable. It contradicts some of our present day ideologies and teachings and how the blessing of God has been interpreted and applied.

There will be those who would suggest that this is Old Testament, the Old Covenant in operation. They might say, "Things have changed. It is different now under the New Covenant in the Age of Grace." I would suggest we consider New Testament Scripture and understanding. Is it not Biblically sound to propose that the practice of Jehovah in the Old Testament is carried out, fulfilled and in a greater way revealed in Jesus as defined in the New Testament.

Jesus our gracious, loving, compassionate, forgiving, righteous and just Savior.

Jesus is:

- Our Provider – Philippians 4:19
- Our Healer – I Peter 2:24
- Our Righteousness – II Corinthians 5:21
- Our Sanctifier – I Corinthians 1:2
- Our Victory – I Corinthians 15:57
- Our Shepherd – John 10:11
- Our Abiding Presence – Matthew 28:19-20

It was Jesus who declared that He had come to serve and not be served and in that same passage of Scripture found in Matthew 20:26-28, He also declared that whoever wants to become great among you must be your servant.

Does it not make sense that He could only make this declaration of truth if it was the attitude and action of His life and ministry? Jesus, the one who came to serve, served well even unto death. So that He could be the greatest, exalted above all others.

Philippians 2:5-11

In your relationships with one another, have the same mindset as Christ Jesus: Who, being in very nature God, did not consider equality with God something to be used to his own advantage; rather, he made himself nothing by taking the very nature of a servant, being made in human likeness. And being found in appearance as a man, he humbled himself by becoming obedient to death—even death on a cross! Therefore God exalted him to the highest place and gave him the name that is above every name, that at the name of Jesus every knee should bow, in heaven and on earth and under the earth, and every tongue acknowledge that Jesus Christ is Lord, to the glory of God the Father.

What a powerful testimony and display of Christ the servant! He blessed us, helped us, and served us, even to the point of dying for us. What a Savior! What a God! How blessed we are!

Another prime example of this in the life of Christ is found in **John 13:1-17**.

It was just before the Passover Festival. Jesus knew that the hour had come for him to leave this world and go to the Father. Having loved his own who were in the world, he loved them to the end. The evening meal was in progress, and the devil had already prompted Judas, the son of Simon Iscariot, to betray Jesus. Jesus knew that the Father had put all things under his power, and that he had come from God and was returning to God; so he got up from the meal, took off his outer clothing, and wrapped a towel around his waist. After that, he poured water into a basin and began to wash his disciples' feet, drying them with the towel that was wrapped around him. He came to Simon Peter, who said to him, "Lord, are you going to wash my feet?" Jesus replied, "You do not realize now what I am doing, but later you will understand." "No," said Peter, "you shall never wash my feet." Jesus answered, "Unless I wash you, you have no part with me." "Then, Lord," Simon Peter replied, "not just my feet but my hands and my head as well!" Jesus answered, "Those who have had a bath need only to wash their feet; their whole body is clean. And you are clean, though not every one of you." For he knew who was going to betray him, and that was why he said not everyone was clean. When he had finished washing their feet, he put on his clothes and returned to his place. "Do you understand what I have done for you?" he asked them. "You call me 'Teacher' and 'Lord,' and rightly so, for that is what I am. Now that I, your Lord and Teacher, have washed your feet, you also should wash one another's feet. I have set you an example that you should do as I have done for you. Very truly I tell you, no servant is greater than his master, nor is a messenger greater than the one who sent him. Now that you know these things, you will be blessed if you do them.

The ultimate model of servant-hood was Jesus Christ.

The life, ministry and teachings of Christ continue to validate and establish the whole matter of being blessed.

For some, it will seem to be an inappropriate interpretation of God and how He relates to His people. God a servant, serving us, coming to me on bended knee availing Himself to me may seem to be too much, too far-fetched and too good to be true. That is exactly right! The truth is that this is too good to be true! Hallelujah! That is the God we serve. He has always wanted this kind of relationship with man. This is His heart. This is how He wants to be involved in our lives. This is how much He loves us and desires to take care of us. We must always be reminded that we do not and cannot interpret scripture from a natural, carnal, secular, or corporate mindset.

For most, the idea of servant-hood is demeaning, down-grading and less-than. This concept certainly does not fit nor can it describe the God of the Universe, the all-powerful Creator God, and the omnipotent, omniscient and omnipresent One. Yet as you pursue Scripture, you will discover this is who He is. Through serving is how He revealed His love and heart for His people. This idea of being a servant and wanting to bless His people per-fectly describes our great God.

This revelation helps us to better understand the action of God in the Garden of Eden, that we referenced earlier, as He was establishing relationship with Adam and Eve. Remember in **Genesis 1:27-28** the first thing He did after they were created was BLESS THEM.

So God created mankind in his own image, in the image of God he created them; male and female he created them. God blessed them and said to them, "Be fruitful and increase in number; fill the earth and subdue it. Rule over the fish in the sea and the birds in the sky and over every living creature that moves on the ground."

What could this have been? What did God do? What did God mean? In their state of perfection and sinlessness He simply availed Himself to them as to how He could help them and serve them.

The whole Biblical concept of Jehovah's blessing revolves around His willingness, desire and ability to help us. To be blessed of God means He is serving and helping you regardless of the situation, circumstance or needed provision. The blessing and help of God can and does impact all aspects of our lives. He helps us by being our provider, healer, victory, righteousness and shepherd. He is ever with us. He helps us in our going out and our coming in. He helps us when we rise up and when we lie down. He helps us when we are in the city and when we are in the country. This revelation and interpretation of God's blessing helps us to better understand and balance how God evenly and fairly blesses.

Everyone's circumstances are different. Life situations are unique to the individual. We all have differing lifestyles relationally, socially, economically, geographically, financially, spiritually and in every way. So to each of us Jehovah comes in, if you will, on bended knee, and says "I want to bless you. I am here. I am able. How can I help you? How can I serve you? What do you need?" He has this phenomenal ability to relate to everyone in their own circumstances and place in life and to avail Himself to be their helper.

Regardless of social status, age, financial position, ethnicity, success or failure, He comes to you and declares: "I am your helper!"

- To the needy He says, "I want to bless you. I am your helper. I am Jehovah Jireh – your Provider"
- To the sick He says, "I want to bless you. I am your helper. I am Jehovah Raphe – your Healer"
- To the weary, battle tired and even defeated He says, "I want to bless you. I am your helper. I am Jehovah Nissi – your Victory"
- To the troubled, fearful and discontent He says, "I want to bless you. I am your helper. I am Jehovah Shalom – your Peace"
- To the spiritually concerned and those who recognize their need for spiritual life and salvation He says, "I want to bless you. I am your helper. I am Jehovah Tsidkenu – your Righteousness"

- To those who are pursuing a life dedicated to God who choose to live wholly for Him He says, "I want to bless you. I am your helper. I am Jehovah M'Kaddesh – your Sanctifier"
- To the wandering, concerned, disappointed, those who feel neglected He says, "I want to bless you. I am your helper. I am Jehovah Rohi – your Shepherd"
- To those who feel forsaken, lonely and forgotten He says, "I want to bless you. I am your helper. I am Jehovah Shammah – I am always with you!"

He is Jehovah. He is God. In His divine love and sovereign plan one of His greatest desires is to be in loving relationship with us as His creation. A significant aspect in that relationship is His relentless pursuit to help us and take care of us.

He presents Himself to us in such a wide variety of ways, assuring us of His capability and availability. So regardless of your present place, your situation, or the circumstances of your life – good or bad – He is your helper.

To you who may be struggling with your family relationships and do not know what else to do. . .He is your Helper!

To you who may be fighting addictions or bad habits and feel bound or imprisoned. . .He is your Helper!

To the parents whose child is wayward and rebelling against God. . .He is your Helper!

To the child whose parents are abusive and negligent. . .He is your Helper!

To the troubled in heart, fearful and you do not know what to do. . .He is your Helper!

To the needy in body and the sick. . .He is your Helper!

To the sinner, you are running from God and your soul is in danger. . .He is your Helper!

To the weary and tired, you are struggling through each day. . .He is your Helper!

To the married couple, business man, homemaker, professional, successful and unsuccessful. . .He is your Helper!

To the student, man, woman, boy and girl. . .He is your Helper!

One of the most under estimated and neglected aspects and attributes of God that is consistently presented in Scripture is that He is our helper!

Please consider the following Bible passages that will value and validate this truth.

Exodus 4:12-17

Now go; I will help you speak and will teach you what to say." But Moses said, "Pardon your servant, Lord. Please send someone else." Then the LORD's anger burned against Moses and he said, "What about your brother, Aaron the Levite? I know he can speak well. He is already on his way to meet you, and he will be glad to see you. You shall speak to him and put words in his mouth; I will help both of you speak and will teach you what to do. He will speak to the people for you, and it will be as if he were your mouth and as if you were God to him. But take this staff in your hand so you can perform the signs with it."

Deuteronomy 33:26-27

"There is no one like the God of Jeshurun, who rides across the heavens to <u>help</u> you and on the clouds in his majesty. The eternal God is your refuge, and underneath are the everlasting arms. He will drive out your enemies before you, saying, 'Destroy them!'

I Samuel 7:12

Then Samuel took a stone and set it up between Mizpah and Shen. He named it Ebenezer, saying, "Thus far the Lord has <u>helped</u> us."

II Chronicles 18:31

When the chariot commanders saw Jehoshaphat, they thought, "This is the king of Israel." So they turned to attack him, but Jehoshaphat cried out, and the Lord <u>helped</u> him. God drew them away from him

Nehemiah 6:16

When all our enemies heard about this, all the surrounding nations were afraid and lost their self-confidence, because they realized that this work had been done with the <u>help</u> of our God.

Psalm 5:2

Hear my cry for <u>help</u>, my King and my God, for to you I pray.

Psalm 18:6 and 29

In my distress I called to the LORD; I cried to my God for <u>help</u>. From his temple he heard my voice; my cry came before him, into his ears.

With your <u>help</u> I can advance against a troop; with my God I can scale a wall.

Psalm 28:2 and 7

Hear my cry for mercy as I call to you for <u>help</u>, as I lift up my hands toward your Most Holy Place.

The LORD is my strength and my shield; my heart trusts in him, and he <u>helps</u> me. My heart leaps for joy, and with my song I praise him.

Psalm 30:10

Hear, LORD, and be merciful to me; LORD, be my <u>help</u>. "

Psalm 33:20

We wait in hope for the LORD; he is our <u>help</u> and our shield.

Psalm 40:17

But as for me, I am poor and needy; may the Lord think of me. You are my <u>help</u> and my deliverer; you are my God, do not delay.

Psalm 44:26

Rise up and <u>help</u> us; rescue us because of your unfailing love.

Psalm 46:1-7

God is our refuge and strength, an ever-present <u>help</u> in trouble. Therefore we will not fear, though the earth give way and the mountains fall into the heart of the sea, though its waters roar and foam and the mountains quake with their surging. There is a river whose streams make glad the city of God, the holy place where the Most High dwells. God is within her, she will not fall; God will <u>help</u> her at break of day. Nations are in uproar, kingdoms *fall; he lifts his voice, the earth melts. The LORD Almighty is with us; the God of Jacob is our fortress.*

Psalm 54:4

Surely God is my <u>help</u>; the Lord is the one who sustains me.

Psalm 60:5

Save us and <u>help</u> us with your right hand, that those you love may be delivered.

Psalm 63:7

Because you are my <u>help</u>, I sing in the shadow of your wings.

Psalm 70:5

But as for me, I am poor and needy; come quickly to me, O God. You are my <u>help</u> and my deliverer; LORD, do not delay.

Psalm 88:13

But I cry to you for <u>help</u>, LORD; in the morning my prayer comes before you.

Psalm 94:17

Unless the LORD had given me <u>help</u>, I would soon have dwelt in the silence of death.

Psalm 108:6

Save us and <u>help</u> us with your right hand, that those you love may be delivered.

Psalm 115:9 and 11

All you Israelites, trust in the LORD—he is their <u>help</u> and shield.

You who fear him, trust in the LORD—he is their <u>help</u> and shield.

Psalm 119:147 and 173

I rise before dawn and cry for <u>help</u>; I have put my hope in your word.

May your hand be ready to <u>help</u> me, for I have chosen your precepts.

Psalm 121:1- 2

I lift up my eyes to the mountains—where does my <u>help</u> come from? My <u>help</u> comes from the LORD, the Maker of heaven and earth.

Psalm 124:8

Our <u>help</u> is in the name of the LORD, the Maker of heaven and earth.

Psalm 146:5

Blessed are those whose <u>help</u> is the God of Jacob, whose hope is in the L<small>ORD</small> their God.

Isaiah 41:10 and 13

So do not fear, for I am with you; do not be dismayed, for I am your God. I will strengthen you and <u>help</u> you; I will uphold you with my righteous right hand.

For I am the L<small>ORD</small> your God who takes hold of your right hand and says to you, Do not fear; I will <u>help</u> you.

Isaiah 49:8

This is what the L<small>ORD</small> says: "In the time of my favor I will answer you, and in the day of salvation I will <u>help</u> you; I will keep you and will make you to be a covenant for the people, to restore the land and to reassign its desolate inheritances,

Isaiah 58:9

Then you will call, and the L<small>ORD</small> will answer; you will cry for <u>help</u>, and he will say: Here am I.

Jonah 2:2

He said: "In my distress I called to the LORD, and he answered me. From deep in the realm of the dead I called for <u>help</u>, and you listened to my cry.

Luke 7:16

They were all filled with awe and praised God. "A great prophet has appeared among us," they said. "God has come to <u>help</u> his people."

Acts 26:22

But God has <u>helped</u> me to this very day; so I stand here and testify to small and great alike. I am saying nothing beyond what the prophets and Moses said would happen

II Timothy 1:14

Guard the good deposit that was entrusted to you—guard it with the <u>help</u> of the Holy Spirit who lives in us.

Hebrews 4:16

Let us then approach God's throne of grace with confidence, so that we may receive mercy and find grace to <u>help</u> us in our time of need.

Hebrews 13:6

So we say with confidence, "The Lord is my <u>helper</u>; I will not be afraid. What can mere mortals do to me?"

We can begin to see more clearly the true meaning of what it means to be blessed by God as we discover its reality through the Word. The blessing of God, as we have previously discussed, cannot and should not be confined or relegated to just natural things, possessions, and the tangible. The blessings of God effect and impact all aspects of our lives. This gives clear evidence of the equality, balance and purity of God's original purpose in blessing His people.

We must always keep in mind that God's blessing and help can never be separated from the purpose of God on earth and in our lives. The primary result of God's blessing is for the redemption of the individual and mankind. We also need to be reminded that the blessing and help of God is so often connected with our level of faith and obedience to Him. The provision often flows from our ability and willingness to believe and obey.

Once again we reference the words of the Psalmist and the author of the Book of Hebrews.

Psalm 46:1

God is our refuge and strength, an ever-present <u>help</u> in trouble.

Hebrews 13:6

So we say with confidence, "The Lord is my <u>helper</u>; I will not be afraid. What can mere mortals do to me?"

He is our Helper! Hallelujah!

How can He bless and help you? What do you need? How can He serve you?

I recently heard of a survey that was taken in regards to what man struggles with asking for the most. The top two responses:

- Forgive me. . .
- Help me. . .

For many people, asking for help proves to be a very difficult challenge. This often carries over into our relationship with God.

Be assured that He is willing, ready and able to help you. Again, we visit Psalm 46:1. God is an ever-present help. He is always present and He can always help.

Let us look back to our primary subject and text in Numbers 6:22-26. The blessing of God is a direct reflection of God's desire to help His people. What a gracious, compassionate, loving, caring, forgiving, righteous, just and benevolent God. He is committed to us and is always working on our behalf.

The Hebrew word "*bless*" conveys the idea of being strengthened in our weaknesses, compensated with divine ability and provision. His empowerment to be able to do what is not within our own capacity or capabilities. The blessing of God is His goodness in action. The blessing of God is His being active in our lives.

Having established a better understanding of Jehovah's intent and the Biblical concept of blessing, we can now investigate the various aspects of this passage in Numbers 6 and better receive what God was imparting to His people.

Let us be reminded of the setting. The Children of Israel are in the early days of their adventurous journey across the wilderness. Many will die. They will all suffer severe diffi-culties and circumstances. They will encounter opposition from within and without. They will be severely tested in every aspect of life. Their march across the desert would produce testimony of great victories and devastating defeats. Two of their greatest enemies would be doubt and fear.

It is amazing how similar their story paral-lels with ours. The Bible clearly instructs and warns us to allow that season of Israel's history to be an example and lesson for us.

I Corinthians 10:1-13

For I do not want you to be ignorant of the fact, brothers and sisters, that our ancestors were all under the cloud and that they all passed through the sea. They were all baptized into Moses in the cloud and in the sea. They all ate the same spiritual food and drank the same spiritual drink; for they drank from the spiritual rock that accompanied them, and that rock was Christ. Nevertheless,

God was not pleased with most of them; their bodies were scattered in the wilderness. Now these things occurred as examples to keep us from setting our hearts on evil things as they did. Do not be idolaters, as some of them were; as it is written: "The people sat down to eat and drink and got up to indulge in revelry". We should not commit sexual immorality, as some of them did—and in one day twenty-three thousand of them died. We should not test Christ, as some of them did—and were killed by snakes. And do not grumble, as some of them did—and were killed by the destroying angel. These things happened to them as examples and were written down as warnings for us, on whom the culmination of the ages has come. So, if you think you are standing firm, be careful that you don't fall! No temptation has overtaken you except what is common to mankind. And God is faithful; he will not let you be tempted beyond what you can bear. But when you are tempted, he will also provide a way out so that you can endure it.

In Numbers 6, the Lord / Jehovah knew what they would experience, He made this very aggressive effort to assure them of His presence, power and provision. Regardless of what they would encounter and what their travel would produce, He promised provision even before the need was upon them.

What a mighty God we serve! His love, concern and care is so obvious in this declaration and impartation over His children.

The Bible clearly teaches us that God knows. He knows the end from the beginning. He knows what we have need of even before we ask. He knows what our todays and all of our tomorrows hold. He has positioned Himself and promised to bless us, to take care of His own. So before we even encounter whatever our days may unfold, He is already enough! He is our sufficiency, supply, resource, provider, enabler and so much more. He has committed to serve us and remains ready to do so as we give Him opportunity through our faith and obedience.

Take notice of God's determined actions as they are revealed in **Numbers 6:24-26**:

"""The LORD bless you and keep you; the LORD make his face shine on you and be gracious to you; the LORD turn his face toward you and give you peace."'

- The Lord / Jehovah bless you
- The Lord / Jehovah keep you
- The Lord / Jehovah make His face shine upon you
- The Lord / Jehovah be gracious to you
- The Lord / Jehovah turn His face toward you
- The Lord / Jehovah give you peace

Note that the promises of Jehovah here are targeted to both the corporate body and the individual.

His instruction was: "This is how you are to bless the <u>Israelites</u>, the whole body of people." Then He directs the specific provision to the individual. "The Lord bless <u>you</u>, keep <u>you</u>. . ."

This reminds us of God's care and concern for the greater whole, but also of His love and provision for the individual, the one, you and I.

Be comforted in knowing that yes, God so loved the world! Yet, he has the very hairs of your head numbered. Our Jehovah is touched by the feeling of your infirmities. He is a God for all, but He is a personal God. My God! There are so many places in Scripture that give us full evidence of God's involvement in our individual lives. One of my favorite passages to inform and validate this is Psalm 139. I want you to read the following verses from this Psalm and recognize how aggressively involved God is in your life.

Psalm 139:1-18

*You have searched me, L*ORD*, and you know me. You know when I sit and when I rise; you perceive my thoughts from afar. You discern my going out and my lying down; you are familiar with all my ways. Before a word is on my tongue you, L*ORD*, know it completely. You hem me in behind and before, and you lay your hand upon me. Such knowledge is too wonderful for me, too lofty for me to attain. Where can I go from your Spirit? Where can I flee from your presence? If I go up to the heavens, you are there; if I make my bed* *in the depths, you are there. If I rise on the wings of the dawn, if I settle on the far side of the sea, even there your hand will guide me, your right hand will hold me fast. If I say, "Surely the darkness will hide me and the light become night around me," even the darkness will not be dark to you; the night will shine like the day, for darkness is as light to you. For you created my inmost being; you knit me together in my mother's womb. I praise you because I am fearfully and wonderfully made; your works are wonderful, I know that full well. My frame was not hidden from you when I was made in the secret place, when I was woven together in the depths of the earth. Your eyes saw my unformed body; all the days ordained for me were written in your book before one of them came to be. How precious to me are your thoughts, God! How vast is the sum of them! Were I to count them, they would outnumber the grains of sand—when I awake, I am still with you.*

He knows all about you, even to the extent of knowing your thoughts and what you are going to say before you speak.

Amazing!

He is always with you. You cannot escape His presence.

He intricately and intentionally created you. You are custom made by God, His design.

According to verse 16, he has a book written about you. You have made the library of heaven and there is a book written about your life and God is the author. He knew you before you were born and He has a specific plan and destiny for your life. He wants to bless you, serve you and help you to live your life as He has drafted it in the book He wrote about you.

My prayer for you is that you will live every day as He already has it scripted and determined for your life. The beauty of this is that He is all wise, all knowing and He knows what's best for you. To seal this matter, He wants only what's best for you and He is committed to your good and he is working on your behalf.

He is available and wants to bless and help you every day and in every way! There is no God like our God!

Chapter 4

The Shepherd

Numbers 6:22-26

The LORD said to Moses, "Tell Aaron and his sons, 'This is how you are to bless the Israelites. Say to them: """The LORD bless you and keep you; the LORD make his face shine on you and be gracious to you; the LORD turn his face toward you and give you peace."'

L et us continue dissecting the various aspects of Jehovah's Blessing as we further investigate His heart and plan.

The Lord said to Moses. . .

The process of communication begins with the Lord Jehovah as he speaks to and instructs Moses.

It is a joy to recognize that we have a God who speaks. God is not silent. Our whole introduction to God begins by His speaking. Genesis chapter 1 verses 3, 6, 9, 11, 14, 20, 24 and 29 carry the message "And God said. . ." as a result, the heavens and earth were created and completed.

When God speaks, things happen. The power of His voice and His words demand attention. It was and remains to be a consistent activity of God to speak.

We discover God speaking throughout Scripture. . .

- God spoke to Adam, Eve, Cain, Noah
- God spoke to Abraham, Isaac, Jacob
- God spoke to Moses, Aaron, Joshua, Gideon
- God spoke to the Prophets, Priests and Kings

On several occasions in the writing of the Prophets, God declares Himself as the only true God. This was done in comparison with the false idols of that day; idols made of wood and stone. Figures that had legs but could not walk, ears but could not hear and mouths but could not speak. Jehovah God is a God who hears and who can speak. He has spoken throughout recorded history. God still speaks today and in a variety of ways. The Word of God – the Bible is the voice of God. It is His words given to us full of life and power.

Hebrews 4:12-13

For the word of God is alive and active. Sharper than any double- edged sword, it penetrates even to dividing soul and spirit, joints and marrow; it judges the thoughts and attitudes of the heart. Nothing in all creation is hidden from

God's sight. Everything is uncovered and laid bare before the eyes of him to whom we must give account.

God speaks today through the work of the Holy Spirit, through Godly counsel, through visions and dreams, through angelic visitation, through life's circumstances. God is not silent.

God wants to speak to you through this text. The next aspect of this passage is, "Tell Aaron and his sons, 'This is how you are to bless the Israelites. Say to them:. . .'"

Moses, God's chosen leader is informed to instruct Aaron the High Priest and his sons how to do God's bidding.

The Priests were of tremendous significance in the order of God. They were divinely chosen and appointed.

Exodus 28:1

"Have Aaron your brother brought to you from among the Israelites, along with his sons Nadab and Abihu, Eleazar and Ithamar, so they may serve me as priests.

Exodus 40:12-14

"Bring Aaron and his sons to the entrance to the tent of meeting and wash them with water. Then dress Aaron in the sacred garments, anoint him and consecrate him so he may serve me as priest. Bring his sons and dress them in tunics.

Hebrews 5:1-4

Every high priest is selected from among the people and is appointed to represent the people in matters related to God, to offer gifts and sacrifices for sins. He is able to deal gently with those who are ignorant and are going astray, since he himself is subject to weakness. This is why he has to offer sacrifices for his own sins, as well as for the sins of the people. And no one takes this honor on himself, but he receives it when called by God, just as Aaron was.

They were separated unto the duty of representing God to man and man to God. They were mediators in God's plan for the people of Israel. The Priests were highly regarded and they were responsible for the order and activities of the tabernacle, law and sacrifices.

When the Priests spoke to and over the congregation, they were doing so on God's behalf.

Deuteronomy 21:5

The Levitical priests shall step forward, for the LORD your God has chosen them to minister and to pronounce blessings in the name of the LORD and to decide all cases of dispute and assault.

So we see here that Jehovah is instructing His chosen leaders to properly represent Him and to declare and pronounce this blessing.

Numbers 6:24 <u>The Lord bless you</u>. . .

This is the initial provision of Jehovah's Blessing.

Jehovah, again reminding you that this is the redemptive, relational name of God.

It is His determination and desire to bless, serve and help His people.

This is the basis and foundation upon which He wants to establish His relationship with the Children of Israel and as a result models His intent for generations to come. This declaration to bless exposes His heart and desire towards those He loves so much.

The fullness of this message to bless His people encompasses all aspects of God's attributes and relational characteristics. It serves as the cornerstone for all of the other aspects of this impartation.

We could define from this being the initial expression of this communication. That He was saying to them, "Everything else that follows is but an explanation, continuation and demonstration of My intent to bless you."

God presents His ability and desire to bless, serve and help us by His unconditional love for us.

God presents His ability and desire to bless, serve and help us by His divine protection and care for us.

God presents His ability and desire to bless, serve and help us by His grace and favor toward us.

God presents His ability and desire to bless, serve and help us by His peace and wholeness offered to us.

God presents His ability and desire to bless, serve and help us by His capacity to heal and sustain us.

God presents His ability and desire to bless, serve and help us by His wanting to give us security and victory.

God presents His ability and desire to bless, serve and help us by His inclination to meet our every need.

God presents His ability and desire to bless, serve and help us by His promise to be with us and never leave us.

God presents His ability and desire to bless, serve and help us through the impartation of His salvation and righteousness.

God presents His ability and desire to bless, serve and help us by His faithfulness.

This list, though it is not exhaustive, helps us to grasp the wide expanse of God's promises, provision and service to those He calls His own.

This can help us in better understanding how the God of Heaven and Earth, the Omnipotent, Omniscient, and Omni-Present God wants to be involved in your life. Before expressing and releasing any other aspects of His promise and provision through this powerful impartation, He first of all wanted to establish and solidify the fact that He is committed to wanting and willing to bless, Serve and help those to whom this blessing would be presented.

Jehovah is saying, "Not only am I the Great I Am, but I am intentionally with you and I am here for you. What do you need? I am at your service. For My desire is to bless, help and serve you!"

It is my understanding and Scriptural confidence that this is what He is saying to you today.

"I, Jehovah, bless you! What do you need? How can I help you? In what way can I serve you? I make myself available to you. My action is to come, kneel before you, look into your eyes and say 'I am here for you'."

I have and will consistently repeat these types of observations and practical applications because of my intent to change our paradigm on what the blessing of God really means. Jehovah's Blessing is not being blessed by God that only revolves around our personal prosperity. It is centered totally on His presence and provision in your life. How He avails Himself to you and to serve you and help you!

The Scripture is filled with example after example of God fulfilling His promise and pleasure to bless, serve, and help His people. From Genesis to Revelation, God has always been on sight to serve and help those who will look to and trust Him.

Take a few moments for yourself and go on a Scriptural journey and consider God's blessing from this perspective.

Again we must confess that the true meaning of the Biblical subject of blessing is an amazing revelation of our great God and His heart and desire toward us. What a mighty God we serve!

Let us continue researching the ongoing ingredients of Jehovah's declaration over the Children of Israel.

Numbers 6:24

*Say to them: """The L*ORD *bless you **and keep you**"'*

It is vitally important that we recognize the reality that so much of the depth and content of this passage is unfortunately lost in the translation. How true this is in the three simple words which are now our focus: ***and keep you***.

The Hebrew language in this passage carries with them a much deeper and powerful message than the translation provides. The imagery carried a significant aspect of the desired meaning and message of the original language. We have seen this with emphasis as we discovered the depth behind the Hebrew word for bless, which is *barak*. With the words being presented, there is an accompanying action that helps the reader and receiver better understand the full intent of the communication.

The word "*keep*" in this text, as well as in many other Biblical passages, is the Hebrew word *SHAMAR*.

Shamar: To keep, guard, protect, to retain possession of, keep watch, preserve, secure, and give oversight to, to watch over with great care.

The word *shamar* is used over 400 times in the scripture and has a variety of applications.

It covers the actions of individuals as noted in Genesis 4:9. Cain's response to God's inquiry about Abel was the infamous statement "Am I my brother's keeper/*shamar*?" This word also describes the actions of the Watchmen on the wall as they are positioned to guard, protect and watch for the well-being of the city.

A primary use of the word *shamar* deals with the consistent Biblical exhortation to keep the commandments and obey the law of the Lord. An example of this is found in **Exodus 19:5**.

Now if you obey me fully and <u>keep</u> my covenant, then out of all nations you will be my treasured possession. Although the whole earth is mine

This gives us quality understanding in regards to our actions and attitude toward God's Word. We should be committed to keeping, obeying, protecting, preserving and guarding His Word in our lives as well as for the benefit of others. We must protect the Truth from every assault and effort of the enemy to defile and destroy.

The emphasis of the word *shamar* in our text of consideration is taken from the relationship between the shepherd and his flock. The word "*keep*" in Numbers 6:24 is shepherding language. It describes the actions of a shepherd giving consistent and intentional care over his sheep. The primary picture painted by this word is the daily activity of the shepherd leading his sheep in the wilderness providing sustenance and care. Each day as necessary, the shepherd would gather thorn bushes and other available material to construct a corral or pen for the flock to stay in during the night. This would serve as a place of protection and safety from any predators and potential adversary.

From this we see the watchful care of the shepherd on behalf of his sheep. The essential duties of the shepherd are to lead, feed and protect. Caring for, watching over, tending to, preserving and guarding are the shepherd's daily responsibilities. The shepherd must correctly and faithfully carry out these shepherding activities. The shepherd/sheep relationship is one of the most unique and endearing of all in regard to man and animals. It is through this language, this message that Jehovah chose to communicate His care for His people. This was a determined part of His intent to bless, help and serve those He was in relationship with.

He was saying through the Priest to the people, "I am going to be your shepherd and I am going to take good care of you. I will keep you! My heart and action will be to guard, protect, preserve, secure and watch with great care over you."

The shepherding analogy and language is a consistent Biblical theme in regards to how God has defined and positioned Himself toward His people. It conveys a powerful message and serves as a tremendous illustration of how He wants to relate to us. This is an absolutely beautiful and deep interpretation of the heart and actions of Jehovah. The symbolism and message communicated through this parallel has served throughout time as a source of insight, encouragement and understanding as to how God wants to be involved in our lives.

Without question, the people of Israel could very easily relate to the message when He informed them that He would bless them and keep them. They were very familiar with the shepherd and his responsibilities in tending to the sheep. Their history was filled with the nomadic lifestyle of the shepherd. Abraham, Jacob, Moses: all were shepherds and are prime examples as to why Jehovah would choose to communicate with them as He did.

Let us consider this action of keeping and shepherding as it is presented throughout scripture.

The first reference of God as Shepherd is found in Genesis 49 and is contained in Jacob's blessing over his son, Joseph. He recognized God as the Shepherd, the Rock of Israel. In verse 25, Jacob defined God as the one who helps and blesses. It is amazing to see the similarities in this passage and what we have discovered in Jehovah's Blessing of Numbers 6:24-26.

The book of Psalms contains the most insight and references to God as our Shepherd and Him keeping the sheep of His flock. This should come as no surprise in light of the fact that the primary author of the Psalms is probably the most famous shepherd of all time.

The Psalmist David knew all about this occupation. From a young boy, he kept his father's flocks. He understood, in great detail, the dangers, demands and duties this occupation presented. He, like no other Bible writer, would deal with this subject and could relate to God as the Great Shepherd. He fully understood Jehovah's intent when He used the analogy of Him being the Shepherd and the people of Israel, individually and corporately, being the sheep.

Let's see what the Psalms have to say. . .

Psalm 23

The LORD is my shepherd, I lack nothing. He makes me lie down in green pastures, he leads me beside quiet waters, he refreshes my soul. He guides me along the right paths for his name's sake. Even though I walk through the darkest valley, I will fear no evil, for you are with me; your rod and your staff, they comfort me. You prepare a table before me in the presence of my enemies. You anoint my head with oil; my cup overflows. Surely your goodness and love will follow me all the days of my life, and I will dwell in the house of the LORD forever.

Psalm 28:6-9

Praise be to the LORD, for he has heard my cry for mercy. The LORD is my strength and my shield; my heart trusts in him, and he helps me. My heart leaps for joy, and with my song I praise him. The LORD is the strength of his people, a fortress of salvation for his anointed one. Save your people and bless your inheritance; be their shepherd and carry them forever.

Psalm 78:52-55

But he brought his people out like a flock; he led them like sheep through the wilderness. He guided them safely, so they were unafraid; but the sea engulfed their enemies. And so he brought them to the border of his holy land, to the hill country his right hand had taken. He drove out nations before them and allotted their lands to them as an inheritance; he settled the tribes of Israel in their homes.

Psalm 80:1-3

Hear us, Shepherd of Israel, you who lead Joseph like a flock. You who sit enthroned between the cherubim, shine forth before Ephraim, Benjamin and Manasseh. Awaken your might; come and save us. Restore us, O God; make your face shine on us, that we may be saved.

Psalm 95:6-7

Come, let us bow down in worship, let us kneel before the LORD our Maker; for he is our God and we are the people of his pasture, the flock under his care. Today, if only you would hear his voice,

Psalm 100

Shout for joy to the LORD, all the earth. Worship the LORD with gladness; come before him with joyful songs. Know that the LORD is God. It is he who made us, and we are his; we are his people, the sheep of his pasture. Enter his gates with thanksgiving and his courts with praise; give thanks to him and praise his name. For the LORD is good and his love endures forever; his faithfulness continues through all generations.

Psalm 121

I lift up my eyes to the mountains—where does my help come from? My help comes from the LORD, the Maker of heaven and earth. He will not let your foot slip—he who watches over you will not slumber; indeed, he who watches over Israel will neither slumber nor sleep. The LORD watches over you—the LORD is your shade at your right hand; the sun will not harm you by day, nor the moon by night. The LORD will keep you from all harm—he will watch over your life; the LORD will watch over your coming and going both now and forevermore.

The beauty of this language is the promise of God keeping His people and how that is paralleled with the relationship between the sheep and the shepherd. This relationship is deemed more significant as you discover the uniqueness of the sheep and as a result the tremendous importance of the shepherd and his role and purpose in their daily lives.

It has been well documented that sheep are a very needy and demanding animal. They require constant attention and oversight. They have tendencies that lend to their own harm and danger. They have a low and slow level of learning. They are found making the same misjudgments and bad decisions repeatedly. Sheep are stubborn and difficult to maneuver. They are bent on straying and wandering which often proves dangerous and deadly. Sheep have a reputation for being unpredictable and seemingly excel in the unexpected. They are a very restless animal and require much care and attention.

An obvious characteristic of sheep is that they are very dependent. They have extremely limited defensive skills and often prove an easy prey for their predators. Sheep have been labeled one of the neediest of all animals. This gives in-depth evidence as to the important and life-sustaining role that the shepherd carries.

All of the observations and defining characteristics of sheep give significant evidence as to why, throughout Scripture, the people of God, we as believers, are defined as sheep.

Be reminded that in Numbers 6, Jehovah was establishing for the people His decision to keep them and to serve as their Shepherd. He knew all of the traits, habits and demanding needs of the sheep and of His people, yet He said, "This is how I want to bless you! I will keep you."

Let us discover other Scriptural insight and information in regards to the relationship between the shepherd and his sheep and Jehovah and His people.

Isaiah 40:10-11

*See, the Sovereign L*ORD *comes with power, and he rules with a mighty arm. See, his reward is with him, and his recompense accompanies him. He tends his flock like a shepherd: He gathers the lambs in his arms and carries them close to his heart; he gently leads those that have young.*

Isaiah 53:6

*We all, like sheep, have gone astray, each of us has turned to our own way; and the L*ORD *has laid on him the iniquity of us all.*

Ezekiel 34:11-16

*"'For this is what the Sovereign L*ORD *says: I myself will search for my sheep and look after them. As a shepherd looks after his scattered flock when he is with them, so will I look after my sheep. I will rescue them from all the places where they were scattered on a day of clouds and darkness. I will bring them out from the nations and gather them from the countries, and I will bring them into their own land. I will pasture them on the mountains of Israel, in the ravines and in all the settlements in the land. I will tend*

them in a good pasture, and the mountain heights of Israel will be their grazing land. There they will lie down in good grazing land, and there they will feed in a rich pasture on the mountains of Israel. I myself will tend my sheep and have them lie down, declares the Sovereign LORD. I will search for the lost and bring back the strays. I will bind up the injured and strengthen the weak, but the sleek and the strong I will destroy. I will shepherd the flock with justice.

With an emphasis on the Book of Psalms, we find an enormous amount of language giving evidence to God's ability and desire to keep, protect, provide for and take care of those in His trust. I want us to visit some of these encouraging descriptive references to God and who He is and how He serves us.

Psalm 3:3, 5 and 8

But you, LORD, are a shield around me, my glory, the One who lifts my head high.

I lie down and sleep; I wake again, because the LORD sustains me.

From the LORD comes deliverance. May your blessing be on your people.

Psalm 4:8

In peace I will lie down and sleep, for you alone, LORD, make me dwell in safety.

Psalm 5:11-12

But let all who take refuge in you be glad; let them ever sing for joy. Spread your protection over them, that those who love your name may rejoice in you. Surely, LORD, you bless the righteous; you surround them with your favor as with a shield.

Psalm 7:10

My shield is God Most High, who saves the upright in heart.

Psalm 16:1

Keep me safe, my God, for in you I take refuge.

Psalm 18:1-2

I love you, LORD, my strength. The LORD is my rock, my fortress and my deliverer; my God is my rock, in whom I take refuge, my shield and the horn of my salvation, my stronghold.

Psalm 27:1

The LORD is my light and my salvation—whom shall I fear? The LORD is the stronghold of my life—of whom shall I be afraid?

Psalm 28:6-9

Praise be to the LORD, for he has heard my cry for mercy. The LORD is my strength and my shield; my heart trusts in him, and he helps me. My heart leaps for joy, and with my song I praise him. The LORD is the strength of his people, a fortress of salvation for his anointed one. Save your people and bless your inheritance; be their shepherd and carry them forever.

Psalm 31:1-4

In you, LORD, I have taken refuge; let me never be put to shame; deliver me in your righteousness. Turn your ear to me, come quickly to my rescue; be my rock of refuge, a strong fortress to save me. Since you are my rock and my fortress, for the sake of your name lead and guide me. Keep me free from the trap that is set for me, for you are my refuge.

Psalm 33:20-22

We wait in hope for the LORD; he is our help and our shield. In him our hearts rejoice, for we trust in his holy name. May your unfailing love be with us, LORD, even as we put our hope in you.

Psalm 37:39-40

The salvation of the righteous comes from the LORD; he is their stronghold in time of trouble. The LORD helps them and delivers them; he delivers them from the wicked and saves them, because they take refuge in him.

Psalm 46:1

God is our refuge and strength, an ever-present help in trouble.

Psalm 59:16-17

But I will sing of your strength, in the morning I will sing of your love; for you are my fortress, my refuge in times of trouble. You are my strength, I sing praise to you; you, God, are my fortress, my God on whom I can rely.

Psalm 62:1-2

Truly my soul finds rest in God; my salvation comes from him. Truly he is my rock and my salvation; he is my fortress, I will never be shaken.

Psalm 118:6-8

The LORD is with me; I will not be afraid. What can mere mortals do to me? The LORD is with me; he is my helper. I look in triumph on my enemies. It is better to take refuge in the LORD than to trust in humans.

Psalm 144:1-2

Praise be to the LORD my Rock, who trains my hands for war, my fingers for battle. He is my loving God and my fortress, my stronghold and my deliverer, my shield, in whom I take refuge, who subdues peoples under me.

Psalm 146:5-10

Blessed are those whose help is the God of Jacob, whose hope is in the LORD their God. He is the Maker of heaven and earth, the sea, and everything in them—he remains faithful forever. He upholds the cause of the oppressed and gives food to the hungry. The LORD sets prisoners free; the LORD gives sight to the blind, the LORD lifts up those who are bowed down, the LORD loves the righteous. The LORD watches over the foreigner and sustains the fatherless and the widow, but he frustrates the ways of the wicked. The LORD reigns forever, your God, O Zion, for all generations. Praise the LORD.

Before we leave Old Testament territory and transition into the significant teaching and application of this whole subject of The Lord Keep Thee from a New Testament understanding, there are many other points of reference that are noteworthy, but one to which we will give our attention.

Earlier in our writings, we presented to you the tremendous value placed upon the names of God. We now know that His names give us a most accurate way to discover who He is and what He does. His names serve as one of the clearest definitions of God's character and activity. They clearly reveal His attributes and His relational intent with man.

It is very interesting that we again recognize that one of the compound names of Jehovah as He revealed Himself is Jehovah-Rohi. The Lord is my Shepherd. It is obvious that God wanted to make sure that His people understand this aspect of His relationship and service to man.

As we all know, Psalm 23 is the crescendo of Biblical content providing insight and evidence to God as our Shepherd. The God of the universe willingly wants to take on the role and responsibility of our Shepherd.

Jehovah-Rohi, the self-existing, self-sustaining, all-sufficient, covenant keeping, redemptive God is the Great I Am revealed as my own personal shepherd. We are His people and the sheep of His pasture, as stated in Psalm 100:3.

To recognize that while journeying through this world of instability and insecurity that we have Him as the shepherd, who leads us, feeds us and protects us is more than wonderful. How attractive and precious is this promise and how comforting the realities of Psalm 23 are as they apply to our lives.

The questions are often asked, and reasonably so: "In what can you place your trust?" "Who can you trust?" "What in our world today has proven itself dependable or trustworthy?" The scriptures clearly teach against the foolishness of trusting in things or in man's order or effort. Psalm 118:8 informs us that it is better to put your trust in the Lord than to put confidence in man. Psalm 20:7 teaches us that some have chosen to put their trust in chariots and horses but the sheep of His pasture know the blessing of putting our trust in Him.

We are graciously extended the opportunity to rest in the reality of His constant and loving, watchful care and attention. Jehovah-Rohi's love and care for His flock is beyond question. He has proven unequivocally that He is with them and He is their helper. Regardless of the demand or need, He is more than able and sufficient. The Lord is my personal shepherd and keeper! This is another glorious aspect of how He wants to bless and serve His people.

This whole Biblical theme seemingly elevates us as we engage New Testament understanding. Any student of Scripture knows full well the depth and accuracy of this analogy as it takes on new dimensions when applied to the Lord Jesus Christ.

The most appropriate passage to use in discovering the details of this parallel with Jesus would certainly be in John's gospel, Chapter

10. Here we receive the great discourse from Christ on the shepherd and his sheep. In this teaching, He uses this analogy to define Himself and those who would believe in and follow Him. He uses this teaching to present Himself as the Good Shepherd. Twice in verses 11 and 14 He states, "I am the good shepherd." There are a number of very important truths and valuable revelations that the master teacher presents:

- He establishes that He is the gate to the sheepfold.

John 10: 7-9

Therefore Jesus said again, "Very truly I tell you, I am the gate for the sheep. All who have come before me are thieves and robbers, but the sheep have not listened to them. I am the gate; whoever enters through me will be saved. They will come in and go out, and find pasture.

- He contrasts the actions of the Good Shepherd with those of the thief.

John 10:10

The thief comes only to steal and kill and destroy; I have come that they may have life, and have it to the full.

- He defines the care and sacrifice that the Good Shepherd provides.

John 10:11-13

"I am the good shepherd. The good shepherd lays down his life for the sheep. The hired hand is not the shepherd and does not own the sheep. So when he sees the wolf coming, he abandons the sheep and runs away. Then the wolf attacks the flock and scatters it. The man runs away because he is a hired hand and cares nothing for the sheep.

- He explains the genuine relationship between the Good Shepherd and His flock.

John 10:14-15

"I am the good shepherd; I know my sheep and my sheep know me—just as the Father knows me and I know the Father—and I lay down my life for the sheep.

This whole matter validates the primary truth of this writing that it is God's desire to bless and serve His people. One of the primary ways that He chose to explain and present His servant heart is that HE WILL KEEP US.

He is your Good Shepherd. He laid down His life for your salvation. He knows you by name. He is your keeper and protector.

I can appropriately declare the Lord bless you and know that in that declaration and impartation resides His promise to be your keeper.

We will conclude this train of thought by considering several other New Testament passages. They serve as continuing evidence and validation that the Lord is our Shepherd. Let us rejoice in and celebrate this wonderful reality and be sure to recognize how blessed we are.

Matthew 9:35-36

Jesus went through all the towns and villages, teaching in their synagogues, proclaiming the good news of the kingdom and healing every disease and sickness. When he saw the crowds, he had compassion on them, because they were harassed and helpless, like sheep without a shepherd.

Luke 15:3-7

Then Jesus told them this parable: "Suppose one of you has a hundred sheep and loses one of them. Doesn't he leave the ninety-nine in the open country and go after the lost sheep until he finds it? And when he finds it, he joyfully puts it on his shoulders and goes home. Then he calls his friends and neighbors together and says, 'Rejoice with me; I have found my lost sheep.' I tell you that in the same way there will be more rejoicing in heaven over one sinner who repents than over ninety-nine righteous persons who do not need to repent.

Hebrews 13:20-21

Now may the God of peace, who through the blood of the eternal covenant brought back from the dead our Lord Jesus, that great Shepherd of the sheep, equip you with everything good for doing his will, and may he work in us what is pleasing to him, through Jesus Christ, to whom be glory for ever and ever. Amen.

I Peter 2:25

For "you were like sheep going astray," but now you have returned to the Shepherd and Overseer of your souls.

I Peter 5:1-4

To the elders among you, I appeal as a fellow elder and a witness of Christ's sufferings who also will share in the glory to be revealed: Be shepherds of God's flock that is under your care, watching over them—not because you must, but because you are willing, as God wants you to be; not pursuing dishonest gain, but eager to serve; not lording it over those entrusted to you, but being examples to the flock. And when the Chief Shepherd appears, you will receive the crown of glory that will never fade away.

Revelation 7:15-17

Therefore, "they are before the throne of God and serve him day and night in his temple; and he who sits on the throne will shelter them with his presence. 'Never again will they hunger; never again will they thirst. The sun will not beat down on them,' nor any scorching heat. For the Lamb at the center of the throne will be their shepherd; 'he will lead them to springs of living water.' 'And God will wipe away every tear from their eyes.'"

Chapter 5

Grace

In our continued pursuit of coming to a greater understanding of the blessing of God, let us consider the next section of this journey in **Numbers 6:25**.

The LORD make his face shine on you and be gracious to you

The anatomy of God is a very exciting example of how He is presented in Scripture. Physical descriptions are used to aid us in coming to a better understanding of who He is and what He does.

In this passage we will learn about the face of God. We are also introduced throughout the Bible to the hand of God, the arm of God, the mouth of God, the feet of God, the eyes of God and so forth.

The terminology and declaration in verse 25 is evidence of Jehovah's determined efforts to reveal to us His commitment and desire to serve and bless His people.

❖ The Lord / Jehovah make His face shine upon you
❖ Be gracious to you

These phrases are additional promises and provisions that He makes to validate how He is coming to His people with the priority purpose to serve them. The menu of His service increases as He is on bended knee. He is making Himself available to their needs and how He can best take care of them.

Remember that there is the reality of missing much of the content and intent through the translation of the Scripture. We will endeavor to better understand what was on the heart and mind of God as He communicated this to His people.

The Lord make His face shine upon you. . .

The subject of the face of God is very interesting as it is presented and referenced in Scripture.There are three primary themes that are discovered when a Biblical search is pursued.

1. The action of seeking the face of God as noted in the following passages

I Chronicles 16:11

Look to the Lord and his strength; seek his face always.

II Chronicles 7:14

If my people, who are called by my name, will humble themselves and pray and seek my face and turn from their wicked

ways, then I will hear from heaven, and I will forgive their sin and will heal their land.

Psalm 27:8

My heart says of you, "Seek his face!" Your face, LORD, I will seek.

Psalm 105:4

Look to the LORD and his strength; seek his face always.

2. The possibility and reality of Him hiding His face

Psalm 13:1-6

How long, LORD? Will you forget me forever? How long will you hide your face from me? How long must I wrestle with my thoughts and day after day have sorrow in my heart?

How long will my enemy triumph over me? Look on me and answer, LORD my God. Give light to my eyes, or I will sleep in death, and my enemy will say, "I have overcome him," and my foes will rejoice when I fall. But I trust in your unfailing love; my heart rejoices in your salvation. I will sing the LORD's praise, for he has been good to me.

Psalm 88:13-14

But I cry to you for help, Lord; in the morning my prayer comes before you. Why, Lord, do you reject me and hide your face from me?

Psalm 143:7-10

Answer me quickly, Lord; my spirit fails. Do not hide your face from me or I will be like those who go down to the pit. Let the morning bring me word of your unfailing love, for I have put my trust in you. Show me the way I should go, for to you I entrust my life. Rescue me from my enemies, Lord, for I hide myself in you. Teach me to do your will, for you are my God; may your good Spirit lead me on level ground.

Isaiah 54:7-8

"For a brief moment I abandoned you, but with deep compassion I will bring you back. In a surge of anger I hid my face from you for a moment, but with everlasting kindness I will have compassion on you," says the Lord your Redeemer.

Isaiah 59:1-2

Surely the arm of the Lord is not too short to save, nor his ear too dull to hear. But your iniquities have separated you from your God; your sins have hidden his face from you, so that he will not hear.

Micah 3:4

Then they will cry out to the Lord, but he will not answer them. At that time he will hide his face from them because of the evil they have done.

These verses provide insight into God's face being turned away from His people. The reasons for His actions and for showing this level of displeasure are the results of disobedience, rebellion and sin. When His people reject and turn from Him, there is the action of turning His face away.

3. Our emphasis in regards to the face of God as referenced in Numbers 6:26, is focusing on the Lord making His face shine upon you. This is found in several other passages.

Psalm 4:6-8

Many, Lord, are asking, "Who will bring us prosperity?" Let the light of your face shine on us. Fill my heart with joy when their grain and new wine abound. In peace I will lie down and sleep, for you alone, Lord, make me dwell in safety.

Psalm 31:14-16

*But I trust in you, L*ORD*; I say, "You are my God." My times are in your hands; deliver me from the hands of my enemies, from those who pursue me. Let your face shine on your servant; save me in your unfailing love.*

Psalm 67:1-2

May God be gracious to us and bless us and make his face shine on us—so that your ways may be known on earth, your salvation among all nations.

Psalm 80:3, 7, and 19

Restore us, O God; make your face shine on us, that we may be saved.

Restore us, God Almighty; make your face shine on us, that we may be saved.

*Restore us, L*ORD *God Almighty; make your face shine on us, that we may be saved.*

What is Jehovah saying? What is the meaning of this communication?

The shining face indicates God's good will and good works in one's life. It is the evidence of His love, favor, pleasure and acceptance. The Lord's face shining is like the breaking forth or shining of the sun. There are at least two references to the shining face found in the New

Testament and both compare the face to the shining of the sun.

Matthew 17:1-2

After six days Jesus took with him Peter, James and John the brother of James, and led them up a high mountain by themselves. There he was transfigured before them. His face shone like the sun, and his clothes became as white as the light.

Here we are given the description of Christ during what is known as His transfiguration.

Revelation 1:12-16

I turned around to see the voice that was speaking to me. And when I turned I saw seven golden lampstands, and among the lampstands was someone like a son of man, dressed in a robe reaching down to his feet and with a golden sash around his chest. The hair on his head was white like wool, as white as snow, and his eyes were like blazing fire. His feet were like bronze glowing in a furnace, and his voice was like the sound of rushing waters. In his right hand he held seven stars, and coming out of his mouth was a sharp, double-edged sword. His face was like the sun shining in all its brilliance.

This is the initiation of John's charge to write the revelation that he received. This provides powerful insight into the glory, majesty and power of our Christ. His face was like the sun. Wow!

It defines His radiance, light, brilliance, warmth and life giving provision. It is evidence of His power and might, His capacity and ability. The face shining can be simply defined as the smile of a loving and adoring father to his children.

The word *"face"* in the context of Numbers 6:25 carries with it a plural reflection, like the many rays of sunlight produced by the sun. It bears the idea of multiple emotions and expressions. It conveys the picture of Jehovah's multiple characteristics being presented and offered. Remember, this is how He wants to bless His people: by revealing through the shining forth of His face the many ways and means that He can serve and take care of His own. This caring, keeping, gracious, loving and forgiving God; He who is our provider, healer, sustainer, victory, shepherd, righteous, holy, just, ever-abiding and always available God. He now demonstrates His servant-hood by informing His people of His smile of pleasure and favor toward them.

This is so accurately presented in **Proverbs 16:15**.

When a king's face brightens, it means life; his favor is like a rain cloud in spring.

The smile of the King means life. It is refreshing, renewing and life giving.

In the days of true Kingdom rule and reign, the King was the only and final authority. When one was brought into the King's presence and he turned his face away from the individual, it generally meant judgment, punishment or death. On the other hand, when the King would turn toward them and smile, it was a sign of favor, acceptance and life.

Jehovah is saying, "You are my accepted, my beloved. I am yours to provide life and security. I am your God, as well as all you need. My favor and goodwill are released upon you."

It is not because He has to, but it is all because He **wants** to.

Lift your face heavenward. God is smiling. His face is shining upon you. Know that He is working on your behalf. The favor of heaven is promised to you and is freely given.

In the continuation of Numbers 6:25, the literary device of parallelism is being used. The elements are expressed in different ways but with the same determined message. The intent is repeated by using different words and a different phrase.

The Lord be gracious to us. . .

The matter of grace is one of the most encompassing of all Biblical subjects. Grace is a topic that is intensely discussed and pursued but never fully comprehended. It is the message of heaven and the greatest need of man. Grace is the most generous gift of God to man, the neediest recipient. This subject is in the conversation of Scripture from Genesis to Revelation. We discover grace is available to all and is for whosoever will. Grace knows no boundaries and has no limits. The Grace of God has the potential to impact everyone. It is for the rich and the poor, the ruler and the pauper, the learned and the ignorant. Grace can overcome every boundary.

This impartation of Jehovah to His people is another strong and undeniable effort on His part to serve, bless and help those He loves. He is saying, "I know who you are and I know your situation. You are in great need and so My commitment to you is to give freely to you, My great grace."

Through this offering, He is servicing and providing for man's deepest need. Grace is the grandest theme of tongue and pen. The orator, author, poet and preacher have made valiant effort in attempting to capture and communicate its beauty and blessing. Angels of Heaven and Biblical authors have provided insight and understanding to this eternal and life changing provision. It has been properly defined as marvelous, amazing, sufficient, unconditional and undeserved. Grace is one of the strongest and most intentional of God's aggressive efforts in pursuing and providing for the needs of man.

The word *"gracious"* in Numbers 6:25 is the Hebrew word *"chanan."* In its simplest definition, it means to be gracious and show pity. The concept is of one who has a most generous and valuable gift to give in contrast with one who is in dire need of the very gift that the owner of the gift possesses.

The uniqueness of the situation is that the gift needed cannot be purchased or earned by effort or wages, and the needy party is totally undeserving of the gift. Another most attractive dynamic of this scenario is that the owner who is in possession does not use his position in any way to be overbearing, demanding or manipulative, but is totally willing from an unconditional posture to give freely that which is so valuable and treasured.

The owner of the gifts kindness and generosity is the driving force behind the whole matter of being gracious or grace-filled. This gift of God communicates boldly His unmerited, unearned and unconditional love and mercy toward His children.

This is God doing us good and being about good in its ultimate display: not based on what He had to do, but directly the results of what He *wanted* to do. The obvious and often asked question in regards to the Grace of God is: "Why?" There is no reasonable or satisfactory answer when evaluated from natural thinking or human reasoning. It is simply and dramatically the revelation and impartation of His heart, nature and character. It is past finding out. God's grace is amazing!!

Continuing our consideration of the Hebrew word "*chanan,*" it carries with it the act of bending or stooping in kindness and the carrying out acts of kindness. It can be defined as: to favor or show favor, to bestow upon, to give, to be merciful, and to show mercy.

Certainly to those who have witnessed the grace of God, these defining terms resonate in our spirit and produce great reason and motivation to give praise to Him for His marvelous grace.

In this definition we are again confronted with the action of Jehovah coming to us as a servant. The stooping, bending, giving and bestowing are but Divine acts of kindness and redemption from the God of all grace toward us who are least, lacking and in great need. The grace of God is a part of the nature of God as well as the action and activity of God. The greatest manifestation of God's grace was revealed in the person and work of the Lord Jesus Christ.

John 1:14-18

The Word became flesh and made his dwelling among us. We have seen his glory, the glory of the one and only Son, who came from the Father, full of grace and truth. (John testified concerning him. He cried out, saying, "This is the one I spoke about when I said, 'He who comes after me has surpassed me because he was before me.'") Out of his fullness we have all received grace in place of grace already given. For the law was given through Moses; grace and truth came through Jesus Christ. No one has ever seen God, but the one and only Son, who is himself God and is in closest

*relationship with the Father, has made
him known.*

Please be reminded of the driving theme
and primary emphasis of this text. Jehovah's
Blessings! What does it really mean to be
blessed of God?

Jehovah has voiced his intent and positioned Himself to bless us. We have discovered
that this really means that He wants to help
us and serve us. He knows our situations. He
understands our depravity and lost condition
better than ourselves.

He is fully aware of the damage and dev-
astation that sin and its consequences have
produced in our lives. He is grieved by the
separation that sin has caused between Himself
and the highest level of His creation. The Bible
clearly teaches us that God, since the incep-
tion of sin, has relentlessly pursued man with
an aggressiveness to redeem and restore the
broken relationship.

Let's reflect on Heaven's pursuit of mankind
and make it personal; His pursuit of you!

With this in mind, we will travel through
scripture and investigate the heart and grace
of God in action. In the beginning of recorded
history, creation takes place. *"So God created
mankind in his own image, in the image of God
he created them; male and female he created
them"* (Genesis 1:27, NIV). God, in His creative
wisdom, gives man and woman the ability and
privilege of choice. You know the story. Out
of this privilege, mankind makes bad choices
and as a result, we see the fall of man and the

129

perpetual plague of sin with all of its consequences. An immediate separation takes place
between God and mankind. What would God
do? Would He leave man to his own destruc-
tion? Would He start all over? NO! Instead, He
initiated what He continues today: His redemptive plan that flows out of His unconditional
love and manifests itself through grace. God,
from the beginning, proving gracious to help
and serve mankind. It is obvious throughout all
of the Biblical writings that the primary effort
and energy of the Godhead is to redeem what
was lost through sin and disobedience.

We can highlight this through a series of
Biblical accounts, which are obvious indica-
tions of the escalation of God's grace and
redemptive efforts. In Genesis 4, we read the
story of Cain and Abel bringing their sacrifices
to the Lord. Cain's offering from the fruit of
the soil is rejected; while Abel's offering from
the firstborn of his flock – which required the
shedding of blood – is accepted. Here we have
one lamb for one man providing the necessary
atonement for his sins before God.

The journey continues, and the strategy of
God's grace-filled efforts intensifies. We now
find ourselves in Egypt, where God's people
are in bondage. Moses, the deliverer, has been
called, commissioned and sent. The plagues
are being carried out on the land and people of
Egypt. God declares in Exodus 11, *"I will bring
one more plague on Pharaoh and on Egypt. . . .
Every firstborn son in Egypt will die"* (11:1,5) In
Exodus 12, the Lord instructs Moses and Aaron
to tell the entire community of Israel that they

are to take one lamb for each family or house-hold. They are commanded to sprinkle the blood of that lamb on the sides and tops of the doorframe to the entrance of their house. The blood would serve as a sign to God to pass over the homes of the Israelites, so that the plague on the firstborn would fall only on the Egyptian households. So, we now see that the blood of a single lamb is sufficient for the salvation of an entire household. God is on mission and His grace is paving the way for man's salvation.

The place is the wilderness: the passage of the children of Israel from Egypt to the Promised Land. During this time, the Lord provides for Moses a plan and purpose, called the Day of Atonement as recorded in Leviticus 16. The High Priest is to take the blood of the required sacrifice and sprinkle it on the atonement cover in the most holy place of the Tabernacle. This is to be done annually as atonement for the whole community of Israel. The increasing intent of God's redemptive strategy is consistently revealed: from one sacrifice for one man, to a sacrifice for a household, to the sacrifice for an entire nation.

We must continue to move forward in our Biblical discovery. Join me in the land of Israel at the Jordan River. John the Baptist is preaching repentance, preparing the way of the Lord, and baptizing those who heed his mes-sage. We discover in the first chapter of John's gospel that on a certain day, John the Baptist saw Jesus coming toward him and he declared, *"Look, the Lamb of God, who takes away the sin of the world"* (v. 29). The coming of Jesus

Christ, the Savior, is the apex, the crescendo of God's redemptive efforts. The ultimate manifestation of His love and demonstration of His grace toward man and the greatest proof of His willingness to do whatever is necessary to pursue and save that which is lost. Hallelujah! God became man to serve as the atoning sacrifice for the sin of the entire world – not just a man, a family, or a nation. "*For God so loved <u>the world</u> that He gave His only begotten Son that whosoever believeth in Him should not perish, but have everlasting life*" (John 3:16, emphasis added).

This establishes demanding evidence of a loving, jealous God reaching out to and pursuing the lost. He is relentlessly engaged in this grace filled plan of redemption. Christ's ministry through word and deed models the grace of God reaching out to all.

We marvel at the Christ. We marvel at the message He preached, the works He accomplished, the miracles He performed, the power He possessed – and rightfully so. Yet, His ultimate reason for being is declared in Revelation 5: "*You are worthy. . .because you were slain, and with your blood you purchased men for God*" (v.9). "*Give him the name Jesus,*" was the command of the angel to His earthly parents, "*because he will save his people from their sins*" (Matthew 1:21). The Lamb of God was slain before the foundations of the earth. Why? Because God has a mission, motivated by His love and grace. He is on mission. He is relentlessly pursuing the love of His heart.

The grace of God, manifested and fulfilled in the gift, life, death, sacrifice and purpose of Christ, is the ultimate evidence of His willingness to serve, help and bless humanity. That God, through Christ, would give His own life as the necessary price to purchase our salvation, is the greatest demonstration of the gift of grace. The boldest statement of God's gift of grace was that through Christ's death and shed blood you and I can be redeemed. Imagine God stooping down, bending His knee as the ultimate servant and sacrifice to save lost humanity, dying even the death of the cross to serve and save.

Oh what a Savior! God's redemptive plan is satisfied through grace. When we could not help ourselves, in a position of not only being helpless but hopeless, Jesus, the gift of grace, took our place. One of the most famous Christian hymns, written by John Newton, rings loud and clear. . .

Amazing Grace how sweet the sound that saved a wretch like me! I once was lost, but now I'm found. Was blind, but now I see.

'Twas grace that taught my heart to fear, and grace my fears relieved; how precious did that grace appear, the hour I first believed.

Through many dangers, toils and snares I have already come; 'Tis grace that brought me safe thus far and grace will lead me home.

When we've been there ten thousand years, bright shining as the sun; we've no less days to sing God's praise than when we first begun.

Written by John Newton (1725-1807), published in 1779.

Do not miss it. The Lord said to Moses, "This is how I want to bless My people. . .to be gracious to you." He chooses to manifest and prove His unmerited, unearned and undeserved favor to those He loves the most.

Accompany me on another Scriptural journey and let us discover more grace-filled Biblical demonstrations of God's blessing and His commitment to help and serve us.

John 1:17

For the law was given through Moses; grace and truth came through Jesus Christ.

Ephesians 2:8

For it is by grace you have been saved, through faith—and this is not from yourselves, it is the gift of God—

Titus 2:11

For the grace of God has appeared that offers salvation to all people.

Titus 3:7

so that, having been justified by his grace, we might become heirs having the hope of eternal life.

James 4:6

But he gives us more grace. That is why Scripture says: "God opposes the proud but shows favor to the humble."

Consider the multiple aspects of the Grace of God and its place and work in our lives.

- ❖ Prevenient Grace
- ❖ Saving Grace
- ❖ Keeping Grace
- ❖ Sufficient Grace
- ❖ Helping Grace
- ❖ Gifts of Grace
- ❖ Eternal Grace

We have defined Grace / Gracious from the Hebrew context in looking at the word "*chanan.*" To bend or stoop in kindness and favor as a superior to an inferior: God, bending down in character and action, to help and serve man at his point of need.

It is also very important that we look into the New Testament presentation of Grace.

The Greek word for "grace" is "*charis.*" This word has multiple definitions and applications. Knowing this helps us understand the wide place that grace covers and the many ways it can be received and applied in our lives.

- Favor, kindness in action and attitude
- Unconditional, unwarranted, unsolic- ited, underserved, gift of goodwill
- Free gift
- A position of thankfulness, gratitude
- Leaning toward, disposed to, extending or reaching toward
- That which affords joy, pleasure, delight
- Goodwill, loving kindness, love in action
- Generous help toward someone in need

An appropriate way to illustrate grace from both the Hebrew and the Greek position is to compare it to a loving parent bending down, with a smile, and graciously tending to the needs of a helpless child. This so accurately paints the picture God intended as He declared His blessing in Numbers 6. Jehovah said, "This is how I want to bless, help and serve: to cause my face to shine upon you, the smile of heaven. I want to be gracious to you, to stoop down, meeting you where you are and taking care of you."

We must be sure to recognize that the gift and distribution of grace is an activity of God's goodwill and favor. It is the motivation and action of God's love toward man being represented in its various displays and demonstrations. His grace is based on God's greatest desire, which is to be in relationship with man. Grace is driven by relationship. God wants to be involved in our lives. God wants to help us in our place and time of need. God is committed to our rescue, redemption and relationship with Him.

Let us briefly survey a few of the broad and multi-faceted dimensions of God's grace. It is like the breaking forth of the sun. Its numerous attributes and contributions to our lives are like the brilliance of the sun's rays, each one with its own beauty and benefit, yet all displaying the glory, excellence and loving nature of our gracious God and His consistent endeavor to help and serve us.

Prevenient grace is a dimension of grace that is often overlooked, neglected or misunderstood. This aspect of grace has proven controversial and has been a theological point of contention. I have no intent of engaging it from a position of debate or to defend its theological credibility. The whole purpose of referencing prevenient grace is to help us all recognize God's involvement and service in our lives and His pursuit of a relationship with us, even when we did not realize it or were unwilling to admit it.

This aspect of grace has been called preceding grace or pre-regenerating grace. This activity of grace takes place prior to our exercising saving faith. Prevenient grace is the involvement of God in our lives; sparing, pursuing, calling and wooing us unto Himself. This is the goodness and mercy of God at work literally chasing us down and not giving up until we acknowledge our great need of His salvation.

This is the love of God that works in our lives while we were still in our sins. The favor of God that uses life, circumstances, people, the Word and Spirit to draw us to Himself.

Jeremiah 31:3

The L*ORD* *appeared to us in the past, saying: "I have loved you with an everlasting love; I have drawn you with unfailing kindness.*

John 6:44

"No one can come to me unless the Father who sent me draws them, and I will raise them up at the last day.

John 12:32

And I, when I am lifted up from the earth, will draw all people to myself."

Romans 2:4

Or do you show contempt for the riches of his kindness, forbearance and patience, not realizing that God's kindness is intended to lead you to repentance?

The grace of God is actively engaged in our lives before coming to that time and place of receiving His saving grace. Take a moment and reflect back over your life before you were saved and became a follower of Jesus Christ. How often did God spare you, keep you and protect you? How often was He engaged in your life and you were not even aware or willing to acknowledge it? How often did He knock on your hearts door or use the efforts of love, truth and conviction in an attempt to restore a right relationship with you?

This grace, pre-conversion, has been called the hound of heaven; using the illustration of a hunting dog on the scent of its prey and chasing until the prize bounty is captured. God loved you so much that while you were unlovable and unwilling to love back, He remained relentless in pursuing you. Grace was working and active when we didn't even know it.

Saving grace is another dimension of God revealing Himself through the free gift of grace. This offering of grace is one of the most familiar. It is best presented through the powerful passage of scripture found in **Ephesians 2:4-9**.

But because of his great love for us, God, who is rich in mercy, made us alive with Christ even when we were dead in transgressions—it is by grace you have been saved. And God raised us up with Christ and seated us with him in the heavenly realms in Christ Jesus, in order that in the coming ages he might show the incomparable riches of his grace, expressed in his kindness to us in Christ Jesus. For it is by grace you have been saved, through faith—and this is not from yourselves, it is the gift of God—not by works, so that no one can boast.

We identify verse eight for emphasis.

For it is by grace you have been saved, through faith—and this is not from yourselves, it is the gift of God

Salvation is the free gift of God offered to all by the redeeming work of Jesus Christ. It is by grace we are saved through our faith. This is defined in **Romans 10:8-13**.

But what does it say? "The word is near you; it is in your mouth and in your heart," that is, the message concerning faith that we proclaim: If you declare with your mouth, "Jesus is Lord," and believe in your heart that God raised him from the dead, you will be saved. For it is with your heart that you believe and are justified, and it is with your mouth that you profess your faith and are saved. As Scripture says, "Anyone who believes in him will never be put to shame." For there is no difference between Jew and Gentile—the same Lord is Lord of all and richly blesses all who call on him, for, "Everyone who calls on the name of the Lord will be saved."

Praise God, for everyone who calls on the name of the Lord will be saved!

In verse 12 of Romans 10, as this saving grace is presented, we read in this demonstration of God's love through salvation that there is no difference between Jew and Gentile. The same Lord is Lord of all and richly <u>blesses</u> all who call on Him.

What a powerful presentation of the running theme of this book. . .the "Blessing of Jehovah." It is here that the Apostle Paul continues to validate that from Jehovah's perspective there is no difference between Jew and Gentile in regard to His grace and salvation. The same God, Jehovah that in the wilderness spoke to and through the Priest, "this is how I want to bless my people" is now speaking through His servant Paul, a member of the royal priesthood as defined in I Peter 2:9. His intent and heart is still to bless His people so it is here said that this same Lord richly blesses all who call on Him.

Let us investigate further the power, beauty and preciousness of the saving grace of God.

As it is stated in **Romans 3:23**,

for all have sinned and fall short of the glory of God.

The book of Romans also informs us in 6:23, that the wages of sin is death. . .The reality is that all of mankind comes under the penalty of sin and is subject to its consequences in this life and all eternity. There is nothing man can do in himself to reverse this penalty or to eliminate punishment for sin; no good works, no payment will be sufficient, no authority will be capable; nothing. Man finds himself in a hopeless and helpless situation.

We were like the man described in Psalm 40; in a horrible pit with no way out. The more we try on our own, the worse things become.

The deeper we go, the darker it gets. Is there an answer to our dilemma? Can someone, anyone help us and rescue us? Is there a way out? Is there an escape from our place of judgment and death?

This passage in **Romans 5:6-8** provides the solution. Hallelujah!

> *You see, at just the right time, when we were still powerless, Christ died for the ungodly. Very rarely will anyone die for a righteous person, though for a good person someone might possibly dare to die. But God demonstrates his own love for us in this: While we were still sinners, Christ died for us.*

But God! He showed His love, demonstrated His grace and provided, through Christ, our salvation.

As we have previously noted, and it is well deserved of repetition, Jesus Christ is the ultimate Gift! The giving of His life, His being willing to be the sacrifice for our sins, His obedience to the Father's will, His paying the price for our sins, His rescuing us from the penalty of sin, His purchasing our souls by His blood is the apex and crescendo of God's presentation and offer of grace to a needy, helpless and lost humanity. There is so much that can be said about Christ our Savior and this beautiful offering of Grace. We will allow the scriptures to do the declaring. Read and enjoy the following passages that embellish and bring greater revelation to this unbelievable yet obtainable gift of saving grace.

Through the following scriptural presentations, be reminded that this is how God chooses to bless you, help you and serve you. Grace, in all of its magnificent and multi-dimensional demonstration is God coming to you on bended knee asking, "How can I help you?" He declares, "This is how I want to bless you!" Amazing!!

John 1:14

The Word became flesh and made his dwelling among us. We have seen his glory, the glory of the one and only Son, who came from the Father, full of <u>grace</u> and truth.

John 1:17

For the law was given through Moses; <u>grace</u> and truth came through Jesus Christ.

Acts 15:11

No! We believe it is through the <u>grace</u> of our Lord Jesus that we are saved

Romans 3:21-24

But now apart from the law the righteousness of God has been made known, to which the Law and the Prophets testify. This righteousness is given through faith in Jesus Christ to all who believe. There

*is no difference between Jew and Gentile,
for all have sinned and fall short of the
glory of God, and all are justified freely
by his <u>grace</u> through the redemption that
came by Christ Jesus.*

Romans 5:1-2

*Therefore, since we have been justified
through faith, we have peace with God
through our Lord Jesus Christ, through
whom we have gained access by faith into
this <u>grace</u> in which we now stand. And
we boast in the hope of the glory of God.*

Romans 5:15

*But the gift is not like the trespass. For if
the many died by the trespass of the one
man, how much more did God's <u>grace</u> and
the gift that came by the <u>grace</u> of the one
man, Jesus Christ, overflow to the many!*

Romans 5:17

*For if, by the trespass of the one man,
death reigned through that one man, how
much more will those who receive God's
abundant provision of <u>grace</u> and of the
gift of righteousness reign in life through
the one man, Jesus Christ!*

Romans 5:20-21

The law was brought in so that the trespass might increase. But where sin increased, grace increased all the more, so that, just as sin reigned in death, so also grace might reign through righteousness to bring eternal life through Jesus Christ our Lord.

I Corinthians 1:4

I always thank my God for you because of his grace given you in Christ Jesus.

Ephesians 1:7-8

In him we have redemption through his blood, the forgiveness of sins, in accordance with the riches of God's grace that he lavished on us. With all wisdom and understanding

Titus 2:11

For the grace of God has appeared that offers salvation to all people.

As you can imagine, this is not an exhaustive presentation of Biblical references to this glorious subject. It is a sampling of how the scriptures present this great gift and blessing from Jehovah to us.

The grace of God is like unto the love of God and certainly they flow in and out of one another. Grace is an action of His love. It is humanly impossible to adequately describe the love of God and its action of grace. The Apostle Paul, in Ephesians 3, attempted to assist us in our effort to define and discover God's love by providing some measuring tools. He used the terms, how wide, how long, how high and how deep. He was demonstrating in this effort the vastness and unlimited dimensions of the love that God has for us. He then stated in verse 19 of Ephesians 3 that this love surpasses knowledge. It is past finding out. This love is more than we can understand.

My attempt to define or measure grace is simply to take us to the cross and there behold the suffering Savior: the lamb slain, the awful price paid. You can begin to comprehend grace when you understand the cross and witness the atrocity of sin.

> *Marvelous grace of our loving Lord, grace that exceeds our sin and our guilt, Yonder on Calvary's mount outpoured, there where the blood of the Lamb was spilt.*
>
> *Sin and despair like the sea waves cold, threaten the soul with infinite loss; Grace that is greater, yes, grace untold, points to the Refuge, the Mighty Cross.*
>
> *Dark is the stain that we cannot hide, what can avail to wash it away? Look! There is flowing a crimson tide; whiter than snow you may be today.*

Marvelous, infinite, matchless grace, freely bestowed on all who believe; You that are longing to see His face, will you this moment His grace receive?

Grace, grace, God's grace. Grace that will pardon and cleanse within. Grace, grace, God's grace. Grace that is greater than all our sin.

There are so many manifestations of grace and its purpose and place in our lives. Grace: that free gift that through Christ does for us what we cannot do for ourselves. Grace: working and serving on our behalf.

Another aspect of Grace that provides tremendous insight into its capacity is revealed to us through a very familiar occasion in the life of the Apostle Paul.

II Corinthians 12:7-10

Therefore, in order to keep me from becoming conceited, I was given a thorn in my flesh, a messenger of Satan, to torment me. Three times I pleaded with the Lord to take it away from me. But he said to me, "My grace is sufficient for you, for my power is made perfect in weakness." Therefore I will boast all the more gladly about my weaknesses, so that Christ's power may rest on me. That is why, for Christ's sake, I delight in weaknesses, in insults, in hardships, in persecutions, in difficulties. For when I am weak, then I am strong.

Here we are presented with the powerful demonstration of sufficient grace.

Let us begin our observations of this manifestation of grace by briefly focusing in on the man, Paul. Paul had more to say and was used by the Holy Spirit in his writings in the New Testament to provide more insight and revelation on grace than any other Biblical author. The obvious reasoning behind this reality is if there is any Bible character or author that needed grace, whose life required grace, it was the man Paul.

His story is well known. He was a Jewish zealot who was aggressively opposed to Christ and what would become known as Christianity. The following passages give evidence of Saul's (who later was known as Paul) actions and hatred again Christ and His followers.

Acts 9:1-2

Meanwhile, Saul was still breathing out murderous threats against the Lord's disciples. He went to the high priest and asked him for letters to the synagogues in Damascus, so that if he found any there who belonged to the Way, whether men or women, he might take them as prisoners to Jerusalem.

Acts 22:2-5

Then Paul said: "I am a Jew, born in Tarsus of Cilicia, but brought up in this city. I studied under Gamaliel and was thoroughly trained in the law of our ancestors. I was just as zealous for God as any of you are today. I persecuted the followers of this Way to their death, arresting both men and women and throwing them into prison, as the high priest and all the Council can themselves testify. I even obtained letters from them to their associates in Damascus, and went there to bring these people as prisoners to Jerusalem to be punished.

Acts 26:9-11

"I too was convinced that I ought to do all that was possible to oppose the name of Jesus of Nazareth. And that is just what I did in Jerusalem. On the authority of the chief priests I put many of the Lord's people in prison, and when they were put to death, I cast my vote against them. Many a time I went from one synagogue to another to have them punished, and I tried to force them to blaspheme. I was so obsessed with persecuting them that I even hunted them down in foreign cities.

Paul tells how he encountered the Christ that he was so vehemently opposed to and how that encounter confronted him with the truth that he was giving his life to destroy. He came face to face with Christ and His grace. He fully understood how he was so undeserving of the love and forgiveness that God's grace through Christ provided for him. In light of the marvelous work that grace accomplished in his life, Paul became not only a model of the power and potential of grace, but the primary author that would expose and explain grace to all mankind through his Biblical writings. Grace is amazing!!

Galatians 1:11-16

I want you to know, brothers and sisters, that the gospel I preached is not of human origin. I did not receive it from any man, nor was I taught it; rather, I received it by revelation from Jesus Christ. For you have heard of my previous way of life in Judaism, how intensely I persecuted the church of God and tried to destroy it. I was advancing in Judaism beyond many of my own age among my people and was extremely zealous for the traditions of my fathers. But when God, who set me apart from my mother's womb and called me by his <u>grace</u>,. . .

What a transformation, the power of Grace revealed in the life of Paul.

From that background, we witness in this intriguing account of Paul, found in 2 Corinthians 12:7-10, the thorn in his flesh, his persistent prayer, Christ's prophetic and revelatory answer and Paul's new and life-altering response to the power and significance of grace.

The obvious evidence before us is that Paul had some particular issue that he defined as a thorn in his flesh, a messenger of Satan that was used to torment him. There is no solid evidence as to what this thorn may have been; many believe that it was a physical weakness and a possible eye ailment or vision problem. Regardless, the Apostle prayed intensely as stated on three specific occasions for this thorn to be removed. Paul's prayer was not answered as requested. Just this simple fact can be a great life lesson for all of us who pray, believe and trust God in our prayers. The prayer was answered without a doubt, but it was not what was requested or expected.

Jesus responded to His servant Paul in a very challenging and stirring manner. He said, *"My grace is sufficient for you, for My power is made perfect in weakness."* What an amazing response and what a life changing answer to prayer. Paul, often referred to as the Apostle of Grace because of his consistent and high amount of writing, instruction and under-standing on this incredible subject, now is brought into a whole new level of revelation and application of grace and its powerful role in his life. He discovered that grace was ever greater and more beneficial in regard to this particular aspect of his life than the desired answer he had requested. The grace provided is being dis-covered to be of greater value than the sought after results.

From all visible aspects, it would appear that the thorn being removed would be the best solution. Unfortunately, and often times, from our limited perspective and self-centered reasoning, we do not know what is best. How often in our lives, and as we have witnessed it in others, has the very thing we thought was for our good proved to be to our harm and detriment?

But God, in all His wisdom, infinite love and understanding knew much better. It is good to be reminded that He is always working on our behalf and for our good. This is a primary indicator of His commitment to blessing us, serving us and helping us.

The thorn, defined as a weakness, would prove to be a source of strength and an incredible avenue of God modeling the power and purpose of grace in the life and ministry of the Apostle Paul.

Without the full understanding of God's purpose through grace we have the tendency to lean toward and pursue:

Immediate satisfaction over Eternal value
Personal contentment over Kingdom advancement
Natural preference over Divine wisdom
Human reasoning over Godly understanding

The lesson of sufficient grace, in this occasion in the Apostle's life, is that grace is always bent for our good and God's glory.

The answer that was conveyed, the provision that was given to Paul's prayer was the promise of sufficient grace that would prove of far greater value than he could have ever understood or experienced, save for this response to his prayers and the increased revelation.

Paul experienced a great transition in his thoughts, understanding and practice. No longer did he ask for the thorn to be removed, but celebrated it, knowing that what he had deemed to be such a negative and an obstacle, a tool of the enemy, is in reality providing a greater place for the strength and enablement of God's working and manifestation in his life.

This life-lesson learned by the Apostle and for us to gain is that the power of Christ is made perfect in our weakness. When and where I am weak, He is strong! In what we would define as our weaknesses, limitations and deficiencies, lies an opportunity for God to manifest His strength, capacity and ability. The grace that would be provided would prove more than able to help Paul to successfully deal with the thorn in his flesh. The weakness then becomes a place not to disregard or denounce, but to celebrate. This is Paul's testimony in **II Corinthians 12:10**.

> *That is why, for Christ's sake, I delight in weaknesses, in insults, in hardships, in persecutions, in difficulties. For when I am weak, then I am strong.*

The theme and emphasis now is not the thorn, the infirmity, the torment and weakness, but the power of Christ resting upon him. The concept of this power resting upon Paul or an individual as stated in verse 9, *"therefore I will boast all the more gladly about my weaknesses, so that Christ's power may rest on me,"* is the reality of grace covering us like a tent. Grace becomes a place of dwelling that provides everything necessary for the individual to deal with, work through and overcome whatever the circumstance may be. The truth is that Christ, our provision of Grace, is our place of abiding, covering, protection, strength, care and sufficiency! What was deemed as a weakness in Paul's life now serves as a trophy of victory! He now glories in what he was previously hoping to be rid of.

Christ can often times use our weaknesses more effectively than those things which we consider to be our strengths. Without question, as we discovered in this season in the life of Paul, the very thing we would like to eliminate and believe God to remove can become our greatest advantage. Unfortunately, those areas of our lives that we define as strengths, if they are not under the covering of grace, they can become seed-beds of arrogance, pride and self-sufficiency. They have the potential of eroding our trust and dependence on God and our total reliance on His grace, enablement and provision.

Let us be convinced by the observations of sufficient grace that it is but strong evidence of God's desire to bless you and this is one of His primary methods to serve and help you. GRACE!

Please make personal application of this revelation in your life. Know without a doubt that whatever your circumstances, challenges, situations or difficulties that God's grace is sufficient for you. He is working for your good and He sees and understands from a much different perspective than you. He can be trusted to work all things for your good. Yes, we will keep praying and we will keep believing God to answer our prayers, whatever they may involve. They may be relational, physical, financial, or they may involve matters of the heart, home and health. We know that He hears and answers our prayers. We also know that He does not always answer the way we would deem best. Our confidence is that regardless, grace is more than enough!

A final note in regard to sufficient grace is that it is not popular or advised in today's Christianity to admit or recognize weaknesses. It is not the accepted message to acknowledge areas of our lives that would be considered less than. The prosperity theme is that everything is wonderful, we are blessed by God and we certainly have no problems, shortcomings or any lack in any way. Well, obviously, this does not measure up to Biblical teachings. Paul says after the revelation of sufficient grace that he would delight; rejoice in weaknesses, insults, hardships, persecutions, and difficulties. For when I am weak then through sufficient grace, I am strong. Hallelujah!

God's grace is sufficient for you! For His power is made perfect in your weaknesses!

There is so much more that we could present and discuss in regards to the amazing subject of grace. What an unbelievable gift of God and what an incredible demonstration of His desire to bless His people.

We could spend time dealing with grace from the following perspectives. Please read, consider, rejoice and apply these truths to your life.

THE THRONE OF GRACE

Hebrews 4:16

Let us then approach God's throne of grace with confidence, so that we may receive mercy and find grace to help us in our time of need.

GOD OF ALL GRACE

I Peter 5:10

And the God of all grace, who called you to his eternal glory in Christ, after you have suffered a little while, will himself restore you and make you strong, firm and steadfast.

MANIFOLD GRACE

I Peter 4:10

Each of you should use whatever gift you have received to serve others, as faithful stewards of God's grace in its various forms.

GOSPEL OF GRACE

Acts 20:24

However, I consider my life worth nothing to me; my only aim is to finish the race and complete the task the Lord Jesus has given me—the task of testifying to the good news of God's grace.

CALLED BY GRACE

Galatians 1:15-16

But when God, who set me apart from my mother's womb and called me by his grace, was pleased to reveal his Son in me so that I might preach him among the Gentiles

JUSTIFIED BY GRACE

Romans 3:24

and all are justified freely by his grace through the redemption that came by Christ Jesus.

Titus 3:7

so that, having been justified by his grace, we might become heirs having the hope of eternal life.

HOPE BY GRACE

II Thessalonians 2:16

May our Lord Jesus Christ himself and God our Father, who loved us and by his grace gave us eternal encouragement and good hope,

GROW IN GRACE

II Peter 3:18

But grow in the grace and knowledge of our Lord and Savior Jesus Christ. To him be glory both now and forever! Amen.

SPEAK WITH GRACE

Ephesians 4:29

Do not let any unwholesome talk come out of your mouths, but only what is helpful for building others up according to their needs, that it may benefit those who listen.

Colossians 4:6

Let your conversation be always full of grace, seasoned with salt, so that you may know how to answer everyone.

MINISTER BY GRACE

Ephesians 3:7

I became a servant of this gospel by the gift of God's grace given me through the working of his power.

Romans 12:3

For by the grace given me I say to every one of you: Do not think of yourself more highly than you ought, but rather think of yourself with sober judgment, in accordance with the faith God has distributed to each of you.

I Corinthians 3:10

By the grace God has given me, I laid a foundation as a wise builder, and someone else is building on it. But each one should build with care.

HUMILITY AND GRACE

Proverbs 3:34

He mocks proud mockers but shows favor to the humble and oppressed.

James 4:6

But he gives us more grace. That is why Scripture says: "God opposes the proud but shows favor to the humble."

GIFTS OF GRACE

Romans 12:3-8

For by the grace given me I say to every one of you: Do not think of yourself more highly than you ought, but rather think of yourself with sober judgment, in accordance with the faith God has distributed to each of you. For just as each of us has one body with many members, and these members do not all have the same function, so in Christ we, though many, form one body, and each member belongs to all the others. We have different gifts, according to the grace given to each of us. If your gift is prophesying, then prophesy in accordance with your faith; if it is serving, then serve; if it is teaching, then teach; if it is to encourage, then give encouragement; if it is giving, then give generously; if it is to lead, do it diligently; if it is to show mercy, do it cheerfully.

GRACE THE TEACHER

Titus 2:11-14

For the grace of God has appeared that offers salvation to all people. It teaches us to say "No" to ungodliness and worldly passions, and to live self-controlled, upright and godly lives in this present age, while we wait for the blessed hope—the appearing of the glory of our great God and Savior, Jesus Christ, who gave himself for us to redeem us from all wickedness and to purify for himself a people that are his very own, eager to do what is good.

GOD, THE GIVER OF GRACE

Psalms 84:11

For the LORD God is a sun and shield; the LORD bestows favor and honor; no good thing does he withhold from those whose walk is blameless.

So this is how Jehovah wants to bless you: by providing freely for you through Christ the manifold expression of His grace, which is given to serve and help you!

Chapter 6

Peace

We now move further into the Blessing of Jehovah and consider the content of verse 26 of Numbers 6, *"the Lord turn His face toward you and give you peace."*

Another parallelism is presented as we have two statements that are presenting the same intent and truth.

The Lord turn His face toward you. . .

Give you peace. . .

As in verse 25, the face of God is a primary means of conveying the message and heart of God.

Verse 25 – The Lord <u>make His face</u> shine
upon you
Verse 26 – The Lord <u>turn His face</u> toward you

Both of these declarations communicate the goodwill and pleasure of God toward His people. The opposite would be the frown and Displeasure toward the source of His attention.

We must also understand that the follow-up provision helps give understanding and evidence of the initial statement. As we have previously discovered, the shining face is understood when you couple it with acts of being gracious. So in this emphasis, God turning His face toward us is best understood when coupled with the provision of Peace.

The turning of the face toward gives clear insight to the reality of God's acceptance and pleasure with us. Simply stated, God is looking at us and wanting to have us in His view. We are His beloved, chosen, the apple of His eyes and His prized possessions and He delights in looking at His children.

A practical way for me to describe this action and provision of God is through the following simple illustration.

You and your toddler are going to the grocery store to do your weekly shopping. The child is excited and active. You secure the grocery cart and begin to retrieve the items on the grocery list. The child begins in the cart, but then becomes restless and wants to walk alongside you. After much persuasion and with a desire to eliminate the interruptions you give in and place the child beside you. There are detailed instructions given as to how the child must stay by your side and not venture off. You resume searching shelf by shelf, aisle by aisle for the needed items. All of a sudden you hear a scream and cry that rings very familiar. You promptly look down and realize that in the busyness of your shopping, the child has ventured off and is no longer in sight. Immediately you put aside the shopping activity and begin the pursuit of finding the child. You are now moving from aisle to aisle but your interest is not on the grocery list, it is on your child that, based on the crying, is of course lost and full of fear and anxiety. Then it happens. . .you reach the aisle in the grocery store where your child is located and you call his or her name. When the child looks in your direction and sees your face that is turned in their direction, everything changes. From fear and anxiety to peace and comfort. Seeing your face and knowing of your presence produces a totally different action and response from the child.

God turning His face toward us is saying, "Regardless of your situation and your circumstances, I am looking at you. You have my attention. My eyes are fixed on you. I am watching over you."

If you are wandering, struggling, fearful, anxious, needy, lost and hurting; if your life is troubled and filled with disappointment look upward. Turn your face heavenward because He is looking at you. His face is turned in your direction. His face gives evidence of His care, concern and His ability to meet your every need. The turning of His face is defining evidence of the significance He places on His relationship with you. God wants to not only look at you, but He is saying, "I want to bless you, help you and take care of you."

What a tremendous privilege we have to look unto Jesus knowing that He is looking back at us.

Hebrews 12:1-3

Therefore, since we are surrounded by such a great cloud of witnesses, let us throw off everything that hinders and the sin that so easily entangles. And let us run with perseverance the race marked out for us, <u>fixing our eyes on Jesus</u>, the pioneer and perfecter of faith. For the joy set before him he endured the cross, scorning its shame, and sat down at the right hand of the throne of God. Consider him who endured such opposition from sinners, so that you will not grow weary and lose heart.

Receive the following Scriptures which establish peace as God's provision for all who would receive.

Psalm 29:10-11

The LORD sits enthroned over the flood; the LORD is enthroned as King forever. The LORD gives strength to his people; the LORD blesses his people with peace.

Isaiah 9:6

For to us a child is born, to us a son is given, and the government will be on his shoulders. And he will be called Wonderful Counselor, Mighty God, Everlasting Father, Prince of Peace.

John 14:27

Peace I leave with you; my peace I give you. I do not give to you as the world gives. Do not let your hearts be troubled and do not be afraid.

Romans 1:7

To all in Rome who are loved by God and called to be his holy people: Grace and peace to you from God our Father and from the Lord Jesus Christ.

Romans 15:33

The God of peace be with you all. Amen.

I Corinthians 14:33

For God is not a God of disorder but of peace

Ephesians 2:14

For he himself is our peace

I Thessalonians 5:23-24

May God himself, the God of peace, sanctify you through and through. May your whole spirit, soul and body be kept blameless at the coming of our Lord Jesus Christ. The one who calls you is faithful, and he will do it.

II Thessalonians 3:16

*Now may the Lord of peace himself give
you peace at all times and in every way.
The Lord be with all of you.*

Hebrews 13:20-21

*Now may the God of peace, who through
the blood of the eternal covenant brought
back from the dead our Lord Jesus, that
great Shepherd of the sheep, equip you
with everything good for doing his will,
and may he work in us what is pleasing
to him, through Jesus Christ, to whom be
glory for ever and ever. Amen.*

We now have the gift that turning His
face toward you presents. Peace is one of the
greatest of God's attributes and as a result, one
of the greatest treasures He provides for us.

Peace is known as that one desire that
everyone pursues and that very few obtain.

Peace is a very strong Biblical subject and
like unto grace has a variety of applications and
definitions. Here in Jehovah's Blessing we are
presented with the reality that it is an essential
gift that God wants to bestow upon His people.
It is coupled with grace as the two primary
attributes that He desires to impart in regards
to how He wants to bless, serve and help.

The Hebrew word for "*peace,*" which is used
in Numbers 6:26, is "*shalom;*" one of the most
familiar and fascinating words found in all of
the Hebrew language. Be assured that the word

"*shalom*" means so much more than what we would normally define when using the English word peace.

Let us consider the powerful content of this word and the message that God is communicating when He states that this is how He will bless His people.

"*Shalom*" means completeness, whole-ness, soundness, well-being, tranquility, prosperity, fullness, a state of calm, absence of discord. It is readily obvious that shalom is multi-dimensional.

Like unto grace, shalom always carries a relational dynamic. . .it involves relationship. God is defined as Jehovah Shalom, as well as the Author of Peace. So we must fully recog-nize that to experience and receive the peace/shalom that is presented in Numbers 6 and throughout scripture it definitely involves being in relationship with Him.

The shalom of God in scripture is always most accurately defined and determined by the context of its usage. There are scriptural occa-sions when its emphasis would be on harmony and absence of war. Other times, it would deal directly with completeness, contentment and inward and outward health and wholeness.

One of the greatest characteristics of the peace that God provides is that it is not deter-mined by circumstances or the happenings around us. In other words, in the midst of con-flict, struggle, opposition, turmoil and ill there is the wonderful possibility of abiding in peace. This gives evidence of the strong relationship aspect of peace as has been referenced.

In Psalm 29:11, the scripture tells us that "*God blesses His people with peace.*" We witness the reality of this in Judges 6 with the story of Gideon. It is in this chapter verse 24 that Gideon provides us the name of Jehovah-Shalom.

The circumstances surrounding this occasion are very disturbed and troubling. Not only was the whole nation of Israel under great distress and turmoil, but Gideon personally was in very difficult and life threatening circumstances. He was deeply troubled inwardly and outwardly. In the midst of all this difficulty, God revealed Himself to Gideon. Upon discovering God's presence and provision, Gideon received the revelation of God and worshipped Him as being Jehovah Shalom. We read that through this experience, Gideon was transformed from a fearful, defeated Israelite into the mighty warrior God declared him to be.

The peace of God is produced by the presence of God and comes with the provision of God.

He is our peace. . .

Shalom, in its applications and definitions, always implies the blessing of God. Jehovah's intent, through peace, is to help us and serve us. The consistent emphasis of shalom and its work in a person's life is always for the individual's good. As noted, it is illustrated by God turning His face, attention and approval toward you. Shalom is a gift of heaven distributed to those who are in relationship with God and is determined by God to improve your quality of life.

As with grace, we see the same with peace that in the course of scripture there is an increased understanding and revelation when we view these two specific provisions found in Jehovah's Blessing with Jesus and the New Testament in view.

When you are able to consider peace through the person of Jesus Christ, His life and teachings, as well as the insight of New Testament writers, a whole new level of discovery is obtained and enjoyed. The Old Testament subject of shalom is illuminated and fulfilled in the person and work of Jesus.

Let us visit several Old Testament passages on our way to New Testament revelation that prophetically pave the way to illustrate the ultimate gift and giver of peace.

Isaiah 9:6-7

For to us a child is born, to us a son is given, and the government will be on his shoulders. And he will be called Wonderful Counselor, Mighty God, Everlasting Father, <u>Prince of Peace</u>. Of the greatness of his government and <u>peace</u> there will be no end. He will reign on David's throne and over his kingdom, establishing and upholding it with justice and righteousness from that time on and forever. The zeal of the LORD Almighty will accomplish this.

He is the promised Prince of Peace and of His peace, there will be no end.

Isaiah 53:5

But he was pierced for our transgressions, he was crushed for our iniquities; the punishment that brought us <u>peace</u> was on him, and by his wounds we are healed.

We are only referencing the one scripture in Chapter 53 that presents the awful cost of the purchase of peace for those who receive Jesus. The entire chapter of Isaiah 53 demands our attention as the graphic details of the suffering substitute is presented. Jesus was heaven's sacrifice for the sins of the world. He was like a lamb led to the slaughter. Our sins were placed upon Him. He is the very reason that you and I have the privilege and opportunity to not only discover aspects of the gift of peace, but to experience and enjoy that peace.

The next occasion that the subject of peace is presented in relationship with Christ is at His birth.

Luke 2:13-14

Suddenly a great company of the heavenly host appeared with the angel, praising God and saying, "Glory to God in the highest heaven, and on earth <u>peace</u> to those on whom his favor rests."

The angels announced the birth of the Christ Child and made a powerful declaration to all mankind. Through Christ, peace and grace are being given. Note that this is how heaven determined to introduce Jesus to the world as the source of peace and grace. What a demonstration of the heart of God and a compliment to the content and message of Numbers 6:25-26.

The message and gift of peace is one of the primary emphasis of the life and teachings of Christ. He came as the ultimate expression of peace and to give peace.

Sin brought chaos and division to the world. It produced separation and strife between God and man. In the soul of man there is a struggle, a war taking place: a conflict between light and darkness, truth and deception, sin and righteousness. Jesus, the Prince of Peace, came to win that war on our behalf.

Romans 5:1

Therefore, since we have been justified through faith, we have peace with God through our Lord Jesus Christ

This Scripture is a bold declaration of Christ's provision and the gift of peace we have through His atoning work. What a tremendous privilege and a powerful reality we can enjoy in having peace with God. This refers to the results of salvation where the issues of man's sin and God's justice are dealt with. Sin separated man from God and through the death of Jesus, as our substitute and sacrifice, the blessing of grace and peace are ours to receive and enjoy. Ephesians Chapter 2 is a tremendous New Testament presentation of the dual provisions referenced in Numbers 6 and further evidence of God's intent to bless, serve and help through these precious gifts.

Ephesians 2:13-14

But now in Christ Jesus you who once were far away have been brought near by the blood of Christ. For he himself is our <u>peace</u>, who has made the two groups one and has destroyed the barrier, the dividing wall of hostility

For those who have believed and received Jesus as Savior, you are blessed to experience and enjoy the peace with God that only knowing Him produces. There is no other way to be in right standing with God or to be at peace with God than through Jesus Christ the Giver of peace.

One of the great benefits of being at peace **with** God through our Lord Jesus Christ is experiencing the peace **of** God. This Scriptural reality is best presented in Philippians Chapter 4. Please consider the following passage and the environment from where the peace of God flows.

Philippians 4:4-9

Rejoice in the Lord always. I will say it again: Rejoice! Let your gentleness be evident to all. The Lord is near. Do not be anxious about anything, but in every situation, by prayer and petition, with *thanksgiving, present your requests to God. And the peace of God, which transcends all understanding, will guard your hearts and your minds in Christ Jesus. Finally, brothers and sisters, whatever is true, whatever is noble, whatever is right, whatever is pure, whatever is lovely, whatever is admirable—if anything is excellent or praiseworthy—think about such things. Whatever you have learned or received or heard from me, or seen in me—put it into practice. And the <u>God of peace</u> will be with you.*

There are two positions referenced that provide the opportunity to enjoy the peace of God.

1. Trusting in God through prayer
2. Keeping your mind settled and thinking on the right things

The peace of God is the direct result of applying the privilege and beauty of trusting in Him.

Paul exhorts us to not be anxious about anything, to not worry or fret. Through faith and prayer, we have the invitation to trust and rest in God. Peace is the result of having full confidence in God and knowing that He is a very present and able help. The power of prayer contains the potential of allowing us to have assurance that as we pray He will tend to and take care of us. So instead of being anxious or worrying, we can be at peace in Him. Jesus presents the same message in **Matthew 6:25-33**.

"Therefore I tell you, do not worry about your life, what you will eat or drink; or about your body, what you will wear. Is not life more than food, and the body more than clothes? Look at the birds of the air; they do not sow or reap or store away in barns, and yet your heavenly Father feeds them. Are you not much more valuable than they? Can any one of you by worrying add a single hour to your life? "And why do you worry about clothes? See how the flowers of the field grow. They do not labor or spin. Yet I tell you that not even Solomon in all his splendor was dressed like one of these. If that is how God clothes the grass of the field, which is here today and tomorrow is thrown into the fire, will he not much more clothe you—you of little faith? So do not worry, saying, 'What shall we eat?' or 'What shall we drink?' or 'What shall we wear?' For the pagans run after all these things, and your heavenly Father knows that you need them. But seek first his kingdom and his righteousness, and all these things will be given to you as well.

Don't worry! Pray! Trust God! Be at Peace!

There are many Biblical passages that exhort us to pray and trust in God. They give evidence of the wonderful results that this can produce in the believer's life.

The following are a sampling of these precious promises that we are privileged to engage.

Psalm 34:4-5

I sought the Lord, and he answered me; he delivered me from all my fears. Those who look to him are radiant; their faces are never covered with shame.

Psalm 37:4-5

Take delight in the Lord, and he will give you the desires of your heart. Commit your way to the Lord; trust in him and he will do this

Psalm 91:15-16

He will call on me, and I will answer him; I will be with him in trouble, I will deliver him and honor him. With long life I will satisfy him and show him my salvation.

Psalm 145:18-19

The Lord is near to all who call on him, to all who call on him in truth. He fulfills the desires of those who fear him; he hears their cry and saves them.

Isaiah 40:28

Do you not know? Have you not heard? The Lord is the everlasting God, the Creator of the ends of the earth. He will not grow tired or weary, and his understanding no one can fathom.

Jeremiah 29:11-13

*For I know the plans I have for you,"
declares the* LORD, *"plans to prosper you
and not to harm you, plans to give you
hope and a future. Then you will call on
me and come and pray to me, and I will
listen to you. You will seek me and find
me when you seek me with all your heart.*

Jeremiah 32:27

"I am the LORD, the God of all mankind. Is
anything too hard for me?

Matthew 7:8

*For everyone who asks receives; the one
who seeks finds; and to the one who
knocks, the door will be opened.*

John 14:13-14

*And I will do whatever you ask in my
name, so that the Father may be glorified
in the Son. You may ask me for anything
in my name, and I will do it.*

John 14:15-16

*If you love me, keep my commands. And
I will ask the Father, and he will give you
another advocate to help you and be with
you forever*

Hebrews 4:15-16

For we do not have a high priest who is unable to empathize with our weaknesses, but we have one who has been tempted in every way, just as we are— yet he did not sin. Let us then approach God's throne of grace with confidence, so that we may receive mercy and find grace to help us in our time of need.

I John 5:14-15

This is the confidence we have in approaching God: that if we ask anything according to his will, he hears us. And if we know that he hears us—whatever we ask—we know that we have what we asked of him.

The peace of God serves as a garrison and protection. Peace through prayer and trusting God is heaven's alternative to worry, anxiety and frustration. Peace enables us to operate from a place beyond our capacity and control. It engages God in our lives and circumstances. It grants Him permission to be in charge and is the result of a trust and confidence that God cares and that He is involved in my life and is working all things for my good. He has my best interest in mind.

The other position from which we can enjoy peace is in relationship to our thoughts. Paul provides us instruction as to our thought-life and its peace providing potential. We are told to think on those things that are true, noble, right, pure, lovely, admirable, excellent and praiseworthy.

The lesson being taught here is based on the fact that the mind is the ultimate battleground. Jesus tells us that as a man thinks in his heart so is he. Our lifestyle, actions and decisions are direct results of what we think. It is said that we become what we think.

Philippians 4:8-9

Finally, brothers and sisters, whatever is true, whatever is noble, whatever is right, whatever is pure, whatever is lovely, whatever is admirable—if anything is excellent or praiseworthy—think about such things. Whatever you have learned or received or heard from me, or seen in me—put it into practice. And the God of peace will be with you.

There is an Old Testament parallel verse, as well.

Isaiah 26:3-4

You will keep in perfect peace those whose minds are steadfast, because they trust in you. Trust in the LORD *forever, for the* LORD*, the* LORD *himself, is the Rock eternal.*

The primary emphasis of Philippians 4, is that peace is a gift of God that goes beyond our ability to produce or even comprehend. We are informed in verse 7, it has the power and capacity to guard our hearts and our minds.

Think about that. Meditate on the reality of that promise and the potential that peace possesses. This is telling us that peace (wholeness, order and harmony) will guard (keep, protect and preserve) our hearts (the seat of all our affections, passions, will, desires and actions) and minds (thoughts, understanding and decision making).

The peace of God becomes a fortress, garrison and protection against the internal and external actions that would typically produce fear, frustration, worry anxiety and the like.

Throughout the Bible, we are instructed and advised to give proper attention to our hearts and mind. These two seats of ability in our lives possess such great power for good and evil. They demand proper attention and care.

God, in His great love and concern, has, through Christ's victorious redemptive work, provided for us the awesome privilege to receive His peace that will guard and protect these two vital aspects of our lives.

The picture presented is that as a result of our praying, spending time with God, releasing our trust and confidence in Him, through offering to Him our prayers, requests, concerns and needs, that the peace of God will take charge. It will be our offense against the natural responses and results of life circumstances and cares.

Peace says, "I can handle this. Trust in God. He is greater than your situations, circumstances, ills and issues."

Through your released faith, He is on sight and working on your behalf. Peace is the result. God is serving you and blessing you in this marvelous way.

Praise God!

Let us consider other Bible lessons on Peace. . .

In the Gospel of John, we discover that peace proves to be one of the premier and primary messages of Christ prior to His crucifixion and after His resurrection.

John 14:27

Peace I leave with you; my peace I give you. I do not give to you as the world gives. Do not let your hearts be troubled and do not be afraid.

John 16:33

"I have told you these things, so that in me you may have peace. In this world you will have trouble. But take heart! I have overcome the world."

John 20:19-21

On the evening of that first day of the week, when the disciples were together, *with the doors locked for fear of the Jewish leaders, Jesus came and stood among them and said, "<u>Peace</u> be with you!" After he said this, he showed them his hands and side. The disciples were overjoyed when they saw the Lord. Again Jesus said, "<u>Peace</u> be with you! As the Father has sent me, I am sending you."*

John 20:26-28

A week later his disciples were in the house again, and Thomas was with them. Though the doors were locked, Jesus came and stood among them and said, "<u>Peace</u> be with you!" Then he said to Thomas, "Put your finger here; see my hands. Reach out your hand and put it into my side. Stop doubting and believe." Thomas said to him, "My Lord and my God!"

In these passages, we discover that Jesus is communicating to the Disciples a new expression and revelation in regards to the peace that He had come to provide. Jesus was very much aware of the circumstances and changes that the disciples would encounter during and after His death and resurrection. He was bringing them to a place of greater understanding of the relationship He wanted to have with them and the provision and care He had for them. Up to this point He had been with them since calling them to follow Him. Now they would be transitioning into a different relational dynamic and

He wanted them to be confident and sure of His ongoing involvement in their lives.

In John 14 He informs and promises them that He will give them His peace. It will be theirs even after He has gone. He contrasts the peace that He provides with the peace that the world gives. He introduces to them a peace that is not circumstantial and is relational. He declared, "The peace I give you is My peace." What He has, He gives. He came as the Prince of Peace. He came as the personification of peace. He came presenting the Gospel of Peace. The Disciples witnessed Him modeling and demonstrating peace: a peace that was the result of who He was and a display of His relationship with the Father. This peace, His peace He would impart to His followers.

The world's peace is false, circumstantial, situational and dependent on man's actions and abilities. Peace produced by man's efforts and the world's systems has proven fragile and futile. Rulers, leaders and nations have engaged in the pursuit of world peace. There have been peace talks and peace pacts and treaties. The cry "Peace, peace" has been the voice of humanity, but to no avail. Wars, confusion, division, hatred, ill-will and enmity are the ever-increasing results of man's attempt to achieve peace. There is no true, genuine peace outside of Jesus. It has proven itself individually, culturally, socially, generationally, nationally, internationally and historically. A lack of peace finds its root in one reality; the absence of the Prince of Peace. God is defined as the

Author of Peace and the Giver of Peace. In Him is peace and nowhere else can it be found.

In John 14, Jesus announces that He gives to His followers a peace that supersedes and circumvents circumstance. It is a peace that is not driven nor determined by the present situation, natural efforts, nor man's ability. It is a peace that He possesses that He can provide and impart to those who are in relationship with Him.

Let's dive deeper into the **John 20:19-21** occasion:

The Disciples have been challenged. They have watched their leader being killed and their hopes and dreams dashed. It would appear that they are fearful for their lives and not sure what their future will be. They have gathered behind locked doors. We can only imagine that their conversations and attitudes were filled with trepidation, fear and confusion.

"What will we do?" "Where can we go?" "What do our tomorrows look like?" "What has happened to our cause and our call?" "Is Jesus really alive?" "Are we going to face the same punishment that He did?" There were so many questions and concerns and seemingly so few answers.

In that setting, Jesus appears. He came and stood among them! Jesus revealed Himself alive and powerful. He also demonstrated His continued genuine care and concern for them. Twice on this occasion He spoke to them and declared over them, "Peace be with you!"

His first words were targeted to deal with their greatest need. Right in the midst of their terrible dilemma, He not only appeared, but

He imparted the solution to their struggle, wondering, fear, anxiety, frustration and helplessness! He understood their situation and came to their rescue. During this incredible and unexpected visit, He showed the disciples His crucifixion scars. They were overjoyed by His presence and revelation: from fearful and locked away to joyful and celebrative. This is direct evidence and fruit of the peace that He provides.

This whole scene can be applied to our lives. You may be locked behind doors in your life and circumstances; locked doors of doubt, fear, broken-heartedness, loss, bondage, addiction and anxiety. There are so many possibilities and conditions that are real and disturbing. Our lives, as the disciples, are filled with questions, concerns, faithlessness and confusion.

Is God real? Is Jesus who He claimed to be? Does anyone care? What does my future hold? Is life worth it? Can I be free from my sin and bondage? Is there any hope?

Regardless of your situation, Jesus can show up. By His power, He can move beyond your closed doors and environment of fear. He comes with a desire to help you and bless you. He comes with an ability to speak peace into your life and situation. He reveals to you His wounds and scars. He reminds you that He is touched by the feeling of your infirmities. He knows and understands what you are dealing with and going through. He shows up on your behalf.

His message to you is, "Peace be with you." In this, He is saying, "May every blessing of heaven and earth which you need be granted unto you!" His presence guarantees His potential and ability to provide for you. One of the greatest ways that He has chosen to help you and take care of you is to give you His peace.

Receive His peace. Let Him calm your spirit and settle your mind. He is present and He can help.

Another aspect of peace that is revealed in this Biblical account, as well as others, is that when Jesus imparts peace it brings the matters involved back into order. Peace produces order! The testimony of peace is: Now things are the way they are supposed to be. We see that in this occasion, but even more dramatically in the story of Jesus and His disciples on the stormy lake.

Matthew 8:23-27

Then he got into the boat and his disciples followed him. Suddenly a furious storm came up on the lake, so that the waves swept over the boat. But Jesus was sleeping. The disciples went and woke him, saying, "Lord, save us! We're going to drown!" He replied, "You of little faith, why are you so afraid?" Then he got up and rebuked the winds and the waves, and it was completely calm. The men were amazed and asked, "What kind of man is this? Even the winds and the waves obey him!"

Mark 4:35-41

That day when evening came, he said to his disciples, "Let us go over to the other side." Leaving the crowd behind, they took him along, just as he was, in the boat. There were also other boats with him. A furious squall came up, and the waves broke over the boat, so that it was nearly swamped. Jesus was in the stern, sleeping on a cushion. The disciples woke him and said to him, "Teacher, don't you care if we drown?" He got up, rebuked the wind and said to the waves, "Quiet! Be still!" Then the wind died down and it was completely calm. He said to his disciples, "Why are you so afraid? Do you still have no faith?" They were terrified and asked each other, "Who is this? Even the wind and the waves obey him!"

Luke 8:22-25

One day Jesus said to his disciples, "Let us go over to the other side of the lake." So they got into a boat and set out. As they sailed, he fell asleep. A squall came down on the lake, so that the boat was being swamped, and they were in great danger. The disciples went and woke him, saying, "Master, Master, we're going to drown!" He got up and rebuked the wind and the raging waters; the storm subsided, and all was calm. "Where is your faith?" he asked his disciples. In fear and amazement they

*asked one another, "Who is this? He com-
mands even the winds and the water,
and they obey him."*

Jesus commanded them to go over to the
other side of the lake (Sea of Galilee). In the
midst of their crossing, a terrible storm threat-
ened their survival. While on the troubled sea,
and fighting for their lives, Jesus is sleeping.
Fearing death, the disciples woke Him and
sought His help. Jesus got up, rebuked the
winds and waves and spoke, "Peace, be still!!"
The storm subsided, the winds ceased, the
waves settled and it was completely calm. At His
command of peace, even nature was brought
back into order. The situation returned to the
way it was supposed to be.

Now apply this to your life, situation and
troubles. What storms are raging? What winds
are blowing? Are you fearful that you will not
survive the storm? Jesus is able! Turn to Him.
Call upon His name. Be assured that He is not
troubled, afraid, fretting, worrying or overly-
concerned. He is Peace and what He has He
will give to you!

Peace be still! He has the ability to cause
your life to be in order. He can give you peace;
peace in the storm and peace through the
storm. His peace brings things into order and
causes them to be as they should.

The New Testament message of peace is
practical and multi-faceted. In Colossians 3
verse 15, we discover another inspiring and
encouraging revelation of the peace that is ours
to experience and enjoy.

Colossians 3:15

Let the peace of Christ rule in your hearts,
since as members of one body you were
called to peace. And be thankful.

The word <u>rule</u> proves to be very enlightening
in regards to the role that peace can play in
our lives. Rule is the Greek word *brabeuo* and
it means to act as an umpire, to direct, be in
control. It carries with it the responsibility of
deciding, governing and being in charge. Just as
in sports, the umpire or referee is the authority
and settles disputes. It is their responsibility
to make sure the game is played correctly, in
order and according to the rules that apply.

So in our lives, peace, if allowed, can serve
as an umpire. We must grant permission for
peace to govern and be in charge. Christ and
His Word are the source and supply of peace.
Peace is always the result of being in relationship with Christ and His Word being obeyed.
In all situations, decisions and matters of our
lives, we can align ourselves with Christ and
truth and have peace. Or, we can ignore, resist,
reject the authority and place of peace and be in
confusion, turmoil, frustration and disappointment. Rebel against peace and you encounter
the opposite of peace!

Let the peace of Christ rule in your hearts. . .

The word <u>heart</u> in this verse is the Greek word
kardia. It figuratively means our thoughts and
feelings. As believers of the Word and followers

192

of Christ, we have the awesome privilege of allowing peace to be in charge and to keep us aligned with the rules of the game, the Word of God. In doing so, peace will be the result; in making decisions, in our relationships, in every aspect of our lives. In times of test, temptation and decision making, let peace properly make the call. Peace will lead us and instruct us to decide what's right, what pleases God and to obey His Word. Peace will be the result.

When we face life and its challenges and the enemy would want us to make a bad choice, detour from the truth, travel a wrong path, give into a decision or temptation for our harm, it'"s then that peace blows the whistle. It declares that action out of order and gives us opportunity to choose correctly and righteously. Peace is given to serve us and help us to live life to its fullest and to maximize life as God intended.

Peace is one of the most beautiful and dramatic ways God has chosen to bless his people.

Chapter 7

New Testament Impartation

Numbers 6:24-26

"""The Lord bless you and keep you; the Lord make his face shine on you and be gracious to you; the Lord turn his face toward you and give you peace."'

As we have discovered, this theme, emphasis and intent of God is found throughout all of scripture.

One of the amazing aspects Biblically of this blessing and God's determination to bring this revelation to His people is how the New Testament is marked so aggressively with this same message.

Certainly we have witnessed how that Jesus is the essence, personification and ultimate evidence of heaven's desire to provide care, grace and peace. Through the unction of the Holy Spirit and the New Testament writers, we see this theme increase in emphasis.

Approximately 1500 years after God spoke the original blessing to Moses, we see in the New Testament it become a major message of information and impartation.

Over thirty times the Early Church Apostles use the same message to bless the people of God in their day and we know it is for us as well.

Read, receive and enjoy the following salutations and benedictions that are communicating the message of Jehovah's Blessing to us today.

I Corinthians 1:3

Grace and peace to you from God our Father and the Lord Jesus Christ.

I Corinthians 16:23

The grace of the Lord Jesus be with you.

II Corinthians 1:2

Grace and peace to you from God our Father and the Lord Jesus Christ.

II Corinthians 13:14

May the grace of the Lord Jesus Christ, and the love of God, and the fellowship of the Holy Spirit be with you all.

Galatians 1:3-5

Grace and peace to you from God our Father and the Lord Jesus Christ, who gave himself for our sins to rescue us from the present evil age, according to the will of our God and Father, to whom be glory for ever and ever. Amen.

Galatians 6:18

The grace of our Lord Jesus Christ be with your spirit, brothers and sisters. Amen.

Ephesians 1:2

Grace and peace to you from God our Father and the Lord Jesus Christ.

Ephesians 6:23

Peace to the brothers and sisters, and love with faith from God the Father and the Lord Jesus Christ.

Philippians 1:2

Grace and peace to you from God our Father and the Lord Jesus Christ.

Philippians 4:23

The grace of the Lord Jesus Christ be with your spirit. Amen.

Colossians 1:2

Grace and peace to you from God our Father.

Colossians 4:18

I, Paul, write this greeting in my own hand. Remember my chains. Grace be with you.

I Thessalonians 1:2

We always thank God for all of you and continually mention you in our prayers.

I Thessalonians 5:28

The grace of our Lord Jesus Christ be with you.

II Thessalonians 1:2

Grace and peace to you from God the Father and the Lord Jesus Christ.

II Thessalonians 3:18

The grace of our Lord Jesus Christ be with you all.

I Timothy 1:2

To Timothy my true son in the faith: Grace, mercy and peace from God the Father and Christ Jesus our Lord.

I Timothy 6:21b

Grace be with you all.

II Timothy 1:2

To Timothy, my dear son: Grace, mercy and peace from God the Father and Christ Jesus our Lord.

II Timothy 4:22

The Lord be with your spirit. Grace be with you all.

Titus 1:4

To Titus, my true son in our common faith: Grace and peace from God the Father and Christ Jesus our Savior.

Titus 3:15

Grace be with you all.

Philemon 3

Grace and peace to you from God our Father and the Lord Jesus Christ.

Philemon 25

The grace of the Lord Jesus Christ be with your spirit.

Hebrews 13:25

Grace be with you all.

I Peter 5:14

Peace to all of you who are in Christ.

II Peter 1:2

Grace and peace be yours in abundance through the knowledge of God and of Jesus our Lord.

II John 1:3

Grace, mercy and peace from God the Father and from Jesus Christ, the Father's Son, will be with us in truth and love.

III John 14

Peace to you.

Jude 2

Mercy, peace and love be yours in abundance.

Revelation 1:4-5

Grace and peace to you from him who is, and who was, and who is to come, and from the seven spirits before his throne, and from Jesus Christ, who is the faithful witness, the firstborn from the dead, and the ruler of the kings of the earth. To him who loves us and has freed us from our sins by his blood

Revelation 22:21

The grace of the Lord Jesus be with God's people. Amen.

The impartation of Grace and Peace, primarily through the writings and ministry of Paul, became known as the Apostolic Blessing.

May you and I recognize and receive this divine provision and impartation.

These were not just words to open and close the author's letter. They are more than just a hello and good-bye. They contain and possess the heart of God, the provision of heaven and the reality of what we can receive as we are served and helped through His blessing.

Conclusion

We have had the wonderful privilege of walking through the full content of Jehovah's Blessing as defined in Numbers 6:22-26.

What a powerful revelation of God's heart of love and concern for His people. What a powerful discovery in coming to the understanding of how He wants to serve and help those who believe in Him.

The primary focus of this text was to reveal the true Biblical meaning of the blessing of God: to see this whole matter from His perspective and to allow His Word to define and determine what it really means.

In doing so, we had to expose the error and false perception that so many have attached to this subject. The blessing of God in its purest definition simply means that He has come to serve and help.

Once God revealed how He is willing and determined to bless. He then provided various expressions of how He would carry this out and what that would look like. He presented a menu of divine provision that brought to life and light how He wanted to care for His own.

His promised blessing, His commitment of service and help was to:

❖ Keep His people
❖ Cause His face to shine upon His people
❖ Be gracious toward His people
❖ Turn His face toward His people
❖ Give His people peace

Our journey through this tremendous passage of scripture has not been exhaustive but an effort to help us discover more clearly the heart and purpose of God.

He knows what is best for you and also knows how to provide that. Often we are defining life from a present and earthly perspective. We get caught in evaluating life from a natural view and mindedness. We even put God in that box and perimeter of thinking.

God sees and acts from an eternal perspective. He does not function from our self-serving, earth-bound mentality.

Be assured of the reality that He wants to bless you, that He is blessing you. But, be reminded that His blessing cannot be determined by stuff, the tangible, possessions, success or that which is pursued and treasured from an earthly value system. We cannot belittle or diminish God's desire to bless us by determining His blessing based on what I have or do not have relative to this world's evaluation and accumulation.

His blessing far exceeds anything this world can offer. The blessing of God will have access to heaven: and will be based upon the truths of His Word.

Be reminded: the blessing of God cannot be separated from the purpose of God. Remember

Psalm 67:1-2. The psalmist prayed, *"Lord, bless us so that your ways may be known on earth, your salvation among all nations."*

He will, and He does, bless you. His blessing is to be for your good and His glory. All that He does for you is to be used to advance His purpose and to increase His fame on the earth. That all may know!

The final verse of Numbers 6 will generate our final thoughts.

Numbers 6:27

"So they will put my name on the Israelites, and I will bless them."

The whole of Jehovah's blessing resides in and rests upon His name. That is a primary reason why we gave much attention earlier in this text to His name. The variety of His names defines who He is and what He does. His people will be identified by and through His name. The blessings promised are guaranteed through His name. His name provides the evidence and authority of the capacity He possesses to do what has been promised.

We are blessed by and through His name.

There is no other source or supply.

In this closing verse of Numbers 6, we discover Jehovah's final declaration in regards to the blessing that He has declared to be imparted over the people.

He is identifying the uniqueness and closeness of relationship that His whole intent would produce. We know without question that one of the driving themes throughout all scripture is God's desire and pursuit to be in relationship with man. So He is concluding His purpose by establishing the fact that this is what He has greatest interest in. His blessing, care and service to the people of Israel will mark them and identify them as His own. The provisions of the blessing that He chooses to give them will be a testimony, evidence to whom they belong.

The blessings of God serve as the marks of God"'s brand upon His people. His grace and His peace are the proof that we are His. These blessings come from no other source. There is no other supply save Jehovah. They come only from Him and Him alone. Every other attempt is a counterfeit and a vain effort.

His name is placed upon His people. Again, His name validates His person, power and provision. His name verifies His authority and capacity. His name is the stamp of approval, it is the guarantee.

Psalm 138:1-2

I will praise you, O LORD, with all my heart; before the "gods" I will sing your praise. I will bow down toward your holy temple and will praise your name for your love and your faithfulness, for you have exalted above all things your name and your word.

His name and His word have been exalted above all things.

Have you been marked by His name? Are you identified through His blessings to bear

His name? Has His work in your life produced the evidence that you are His and He is yours? Has His involvement in your life, through His service to you of keeping you and giving you grace and peace branded you as His own?

He wants more than anything else to be in this level of relationship with you. He desires to bless you!

Whatever His name identifies Him to be, everything He is able to do is ours to receive and enjoy.

- ❖ Blessed be the Name of the Lord. . .
- ❖ Hallowed be His Name. . .
- ❖ Call upon the Name of the Lord and you shall be saved!
- ❖ His name is a strong tower. . .
- ❖ He places His name upon us. . .we are called by His name.
- ❖ His name is above every name.

Remember the compound names of Jehovah. He places these names upon you.

He will bless you!!

Numbers 6:22-27

The Lord said to Moses, "Tell Aaron and his sons, 'This is how you are to bless the Israelites. Say to them: ""The Lord bless you and keep you; the Lord make his face shine on you and be gracious to you; the Lord turn his face toward you and give you peace."' "So they will put my name